"Dodds provides an essential discussion for understanding today's battles – and tomorrow's headlines – over the scope of presidential power, concisely mapping the contours of unitary executive theory and practice across American history. The unitary executive is 'neither a fiction nor a fact,' he argues, but a political instrument. Enforcing the Constitution's constraints on unilateralism will thus come not from toying with textual definitions but from political will."

Andrew Rudalevige, Bowdoin College, USA

"Dodds' book represents the best comprehensive study to date on the unitary executive theory in American politics. This work is not only relevant for scholars seeking to understand the exercise of presidential power during the recent George W. Bush, Barack Obama, and Donald Trump administrations, but it assesses the unitary executive in relation to the evolving American presidency since George Washington. More importantly, it helps to clear the muddy waters in presidential research by demonstrating how the theory of the unitary executive is distinct from scholarly notions of the administrative and unilateral presidencies."

Adam L. Warber, Clemson University, USA

"What a very fine book this is! To come to grips with the unitary presidency is no easy task. Professor Dodds marshals historic examples, weighs normative claims, and evaluates empirical evidence in his treatment of this important topic. He skillfully demonstrates that supporters as well as opponents of the unitary presidency have reason to be simultaneously cheered and unsettled. I would use this text in an upper-level undergraduate political science course, but Professor Dodd's cogent writing makes this text accessible to an even broader audience."

Barry L. Tadlock, Ohio University, USA

THE UNITARY PRESIDENCY

The theory of the unitary executive is one of the most controversial and significant constitutional doctrines of the past several decades. It holds that the U.S. president alone embodies all executive power and therefore has unlimited ability to direct the many people and institutions within the federal government's vast executive branch. It thus justifies the president's prerogative to organize the executive branch and to direct its activities, to tell executive personnel what to do and to fire them if desired, to control the flow of information, and to issue signing statements that make judgments about constitutionality and determine the extent to which laws will be implemented. In some versions, it also endorses implied or inherent powers and permits the president to completely control foreign policy and military action.

Proponents say this conception of the presidential office is faithful to the Constitution, facilitates the sort of energetic executive that Alexander Hamilton argued for, and enhances administrative efficacy and political accountability for governance. Critics say this arrangement is constitutionally inaccurate, is belied by historical practice and legal precedents, and is dangerously close to the monarchical power that provoked the American Revolution – and can be especially threatening in the era of Donald Trump.

This book examines how controversies about unitary executive power have played out from the founding era to the present day with a focus on recent presidents, it explores arguments both for and against the unitary executive theory, and it looks ahead to future implications for American politics.

Graham G. Dodds is an Associate Professor of Political Science at Concordia University in Montreal. He has also taught at the University of Pennsylvania and in France and has worked at the Brookings Institution and for a Member of Congress. He is the author of the book *Take Up Your Pen: Unilateral Presidential Directives in American Politics* and is frequently interviewed by journalists about U.S. politics.

Presidential Briefings

Series Editor: Robert J. Spitzer, State University of New York College at Cortland

The **Presidential Briefings** series provides concise and readable introductions to topics of concern to those who have been and will be President of the United States. For students of the presidency, these books provide a highly practical and accessible overview of an important subject related to the presidency. By approaching their subjects from the vantage point of what a president most needs to know, and what the citizenry most need to know about the presidency, these books are authoritative and significant works.

Robert J. Spitzer is a Distinguished Service Professor and Chair of the Political Science Department at the State University of New York College at Cortland, as well as a Visiting Professor at Cornell University. He led the Presidents and Executive Politics organization (formerly the Presidency Research Group) of the American Political Science Association from 2001–2003, and is a regular contributor to various media outlets.

Presidential Leadership in an Age of Change
Michael A. Genovese

Political Rhetoric
Mary E. Stuckey

Making Foreign Policy Decisions
Christopher J. Fettweis

For more information about this series, please visit www.routledge.com/ Presidential-Briefings-Series/book-series/PBSTRANS

THE UNITARY PRESIDENCY

Graham G. Dodds

NEW YORK AND LONDON

First published 2020
by Routledge
52 Vanderbilt Avenue, New York, NY 10017

and by Routledge
2 Park Square, Milton Park, Abingdon, Oxon, OX14 4RN

Routledge is an imprint of the Taylor & Francis Group, an informa business

© 2020 Taylor & Francis

Library of Congress Cataloging-in-Publication Data
A catalog record for this title has been requested

ISBN: 978-1-138-48417-7 (hbk)
ISBN: 978-1-138-48418-4 (pbk)
ISBN: 978-1-351-05278-8 (ebk)

Typeset in Bembo
by codeMantra

Printed in Canada

For Amy

CONTENTS

Introduction: The Theory of the Unitary Executive   1

*What is the unitary executive theory, its origins,
    basis, and supposed benefits?*

1   Nearly Two Centuries of Unitary Precedents   12

*Episodes concerning what would later be called the unitary
    executive, from George Washington through the 1970s*

2   Explicit Unitary Battles in the 1980s and 1990s   27

*Ronald Reagan and the birth of the explicit doctrine of
    the unitary executive, as well as how George H.W. Bush
    and Bill Clinton utilized it*

3   The Unitary Executive in the Twenty-First Century   40

*George W. Bush's vigorously unitary presidency, as well as how it
    evolved under Barack Obama and Donald Trump*

4   Normative Assessment of the Unitary Executive   61

*Is the unitary executive theory faithful to the intentions of the
    founders and the constitutional text; is it good for effective
    administration and political accountability?*

5   Empirical Assessment of the Unitary Executive   77

*Does the unitary executive theory accurately describe what actually
happens in the executive branch, or is practice more complicated
than the principle?*

Conclusion: Unitary Politics   95

*Ultimately, the ability of presidents to utilize the unitary executive
theory is determined politically.*

Epilogue   *109*
Bibliography   *111*

INTRODUCTION

The Theory of the Unitary Executive

Introduction

The unitary executive theory is one of the most important yet least understood constitutional doctrines of the past few decades. It is not some esoteric academic theory of little relevance to the real world. Instead, it is closely connected to multiple recurring debates about the U.S. presidency's power and its proper place in American government and politics. The unitary executive theory is both controversial and consequential, and this book seeks to show how and why.

The President of the United States may well be the single most powerful person on the planet, but the source and extent of his (or, someday, her) power is a matter of considerable dispute. Indeed, politicians, judges, and scholars of the presidency regularly debate the nature, scope, and efficacy of its power. In order to accomplish what he wants to, should a president work with Congress in one way or another, employ rhetoric to persuade the American people, or just act unilaterally? And insofar as a president is inclined to act alone, can he simply order governmental officials to do as he wishes and then remove them if they fail to comply fully or promptly? Questions like these are at the heart of debates about the unitary executive.

Put simply, the theory of the unitary executive holds that the president alone embodies all executive power and therefore is free to control everyone and everything within the vast executive branch of the U.S. federal government, including most of its agencies. Construed broadly, that amounts to total control over some 4 million people (including civilian and military personnel) and nearly 100 major governmental institutions. For its advocates, the theory of the unitary executive is faithful to the constitutional text, it facilitates the sort of energetic executive that Alexander Hamilton argued for in *Federalist* 70, and it enhances administrative efficacy and political accountability for governance successes and failures. For its critics, however, this view of complete executive control is dangerously close to King Louis XIV of France's infamous boast, "L'Etat c'est moi" (roughly, "I am the state"), as if he alone embodied the entire regime and all its powers, a truly absolute monarch. Less controversially, the theory of the unitary executive is in tension with, if not altogether contrary to, the ideas of presidential constraints, bureaucratic neutrality, and policy-making that is inclusive, deliberative, or bottom-up.

Supporters of the unitary executive theory are often called unitarians. (There is no relation to the Protestant Christian denominations of the same name that are monotheistic and oppose the trinitarian theology of the separateness of God as father, son, and holy spirit, though some of the debates about whether separate entities may be subsumed within one are similar.) And the presidents most closely associated with the unitary executive have been Republicans, but the doctrine is not connected to standard ideological orientations, such that the unitary executive could equally displease or appeal to conservatives or liberals.

As an explicit doctrine, the unitary executive theory dates to the 1980s, when it became popular among many members of Ronald Reagan's legal team. Steven Calabresi is generally regarded as the father of the unitary executive theory. Calabresi worked for Judge Robert Bork, for Attorney General Edwin Meese, and in the West Wing of the Reagan White House. He co-authored a book and published well over a dozen articles in law reviews and academic journals about the unitary executive theory, and he is perhaps its foremost expositor and champion. But the unitary executive theory exists not just in academic books and articles; it can be found in signing statements issued by presidents, in various opinions and memos from the Attorney General, the Solicitor General, and the Office of Legal Counsel, and in federal court decisions.

Definition

For a theory that values unity, there is surprisingly little unity among unitarians about a strict definition of the unitary executive theory. As journalist John MacKenzie (2008, 34) has noted, "the unitary executive movement is not monolithic." There is no canonical, authoritative definition, and unitarians sharply disagree about some aspects of the theory. Nevertheless, the following points may serve to explain the basic features of the theory.

Strictly speaking, the unitary executive theory is about executive power, not presidential power per se. But it concerns a vision of the place of the presidency in the constitutional order, viz-a-viz the executive branch and the bureaucracy. Indeed, for some the unitary executive theory essentially collapses the distinction between the executive branch and the president, as if the entire executive branch were distilled into just one person.

After George W. Bush nominated him for the Supreme Court, Judge Samuel Alito spoke about this aspect of unitary executive theory during his Senate confirmation hearing in early 2006. In replying to a question from Senator Ted Kennedy (D, MA), Alito said:

> Senator, let me explain what I understand the idea of the unitary Executive to be ... there's been some misunderstanding, at least as to what I understand this concept to mean. I think it's important to draw a distinction between two very different ideas. One is the scope of Executive power ... the extent of Executive power. And the second question is when you have a power that is within the prerogative of the Executive, who controls the Executive? And those are separate questions ... to my mind, the concept of unitary Executive doesn't have to do with the scope of Executive power. It has to do with who within the Executive branch controls the exercise of Executive power, and the theory is the Constitution says the Executive power is conferred on the President.

In other words, Alito indicated that regardless of whether one happens to believe that the Constitution envisions relatively expansive or limited executive power, whatever executive power it does provide for it gives to the president alone. Similarly, as Alito told the Federalist Society of conservative lawyers in 2000, "all federal executive power is vested by the Constitution in the President ... Thus, the President has not just some executive powers, but *the* executive power – the whole thing."

Alito's above formulation notes the one thing about which virtually all unitarians would agree: if a constitutional power is in some sense executive, then it rightly belongs only to the president. To be sure, many if not most unitarians also happen to have a rather robust conception of the scope of executive power. But the location of that power in the president is primary. Again, the unitary executive theory is not really a claim about presidential power, but rather a claim that the presidency is the sole repository of executive power. The presidency may well also have various other powers, but for unitarians it should have absolutely all executive power.

Beyond that point, unitarians tend to differ about what exactly the theory entails. A basic difference is how expansive executive power is, like whether or how far it extends beyond the specific executive powers mentioned in the Constitution. Most unitarians have an expansive view of the substance of executive power, but there is considerable variation among them on this point. For example, there is a question of just how much control the president may exercise over his subordinates. Can he simply order them to do as he wishes, or merely institute procedures and set priorities and then fire people if he dislikes their actions? Additionally, there is some disagreement about whether or to what extent there may be entities within the executive branch that are in some sense independent or not under the entire or direct control of the president.

A related basic difference among unitarians concerns the types of policy areas that the unitary executive theory covers. Specifically, some unitarians focus on domestic policies and administration while others seek to extend the theory to foreign policy as well. As we will see, unitarians before the twenty-first century tended to focus on domestic matters like control of executive agencies and personnel, while unitarians in the George W. Bush administration also sought to apply the doctrine to foreign affairs and military matters. That distinction has been significant and contentious. Referring to this difference, Vicki Divoll (2013, 152) said, "unitary executive theorists are divided into at least two big camps. And they hate each other …"

Other academics have sought to characterize the unitary executive theory in different ways. For example, Ryan Barilleaux and Christopher Kelley (2010, 222) suggest that it may be seen as a variety of "venture constitutionalism," which is "a form of constitutional risk-taking" that involves "assertions of constitutional legitimacy for presidential actions that do not conform to settled understandings of the president's constitutional authority." Todd Tatelman (2010, 8) of the Congressional Research Service discerns "three prongs" to the unitary executive theory:

> First, unitarians often argue that the President has a constitutionally based duty to provide policy direction to officers of the United States; second, unitarians claim that the President possesses the unfettered power to remove from office any officer who does not comply with the President's policy directives; and finally, unitarians generally assert that Congress cannot constitutionally assign executive powers to agencies or other entities that are independent or outside the scope of the president's control.

And Michael Genovese (2011, 134) contends that the unitary executive theory contains seven basic elements: the prerogative power of John Locke, the energy that Alexander Hamilton advocated, a "coordinate construction" view of the Constitution, the doctrine of "necessity" that Lincoln invoked in the Civil War, the "constitutional dictatorship" that Clinton Rossiter wrote about in 1948, various presidential precedents, and certain court decisions.

Compared to Other Conceptions of the Presidency

The theory of the unitary executive is similar to yet distinct from several other well-known accounts of the presidency. Academic conceptions of the presidency are legion and are usually named after the adjective they use to describe the institution: administrative, cavalier, evolving, imperial, imperiled, impossible, impotent, institutional, managerial, modern, particularistic, partisan, patrician, personal, plebiscitary, pluralist, postmodern, prerogative, progressive, rhetorical, and unilateral, to name a few. Distinguishing the unitary executive theory from all of the many conceptions of the presidency would be a herculean task, but a brief comparison to some prominent ones may be instructive.

In his influential book *Presidential Power and the Modern Presidents* (1960), Richard Neustadt declared, "Presidential power is the power to persuade." In other words, Neustadt claimed that presidents tend to get what they want by bargaining, not by commanding. Insofar as Neustadt's view applied not just to Congress but also to the executive branch, unitarians are apt to resist his characterization of the president as having less than complete control over the executive branch; for unitarians, the president should be able to command executive officials, so there is no need to persuade them or bargain with them.

Another major conception of the presidency focuses on its various unilateral powers. The idea of the unilateral presidency is attentive to the power afforded by unilateral presidential directives such as executive orders, proclamations, and presidential memoranda. Insofar as such directives enable the president to enact binding policies unilaterally, without having to go through Congress, they suggest that a president can sometimes simply command, rather than persuade others to do what he wants. As the title of Kenneth Mayer's (2001) book suggests, unilateral presidential directives may enable presidents to make policy *With the Stroke of a Pen*.

Unilateral presidential directives may be seen as the means to unitary ends, and unitary presidents have often relied upon them to alter the organization of the executive branch, to influence the bureaucracy and the regulatory process, and to control the flow of information. All of those things accord with the unitary executive theory, but a unilateral president is different from a unitary executive. The unilateral presidency focuses on the use of certain tools, while the unitary executive focuses on the scope and location of executive power. Unilateral presidential directives can be potent and controversial, but the unitary executive is a more far-reaching conception than the unilateral presidency, and arguably one with far less acceptance from Congress and the courts.

The unitary executive theory also shares some similarities with what Richard Nathan (1983) called the "administrative presidency." For Nathan, this approach started with Richard Nixon, who sought to use the administrative bureaucracy to further his policy aims, essentially leading by managing. The effort to ensure that the bureaucracy acts in accordance with the desires of the president is key to the unitary executive, and the administrative presidency may be seen as a precursor to the unitary executive. But the unitary executive theory is much broader and more ambitious than the administrative presidency, as the unitary executive envisions more complete presidential control of the entire executive branch.

For its critics, the unitary executive theory may be seen as just one manifestation of the broader trend whereby the presidency has grown in power in both absolute and relative terms, perhaps too much so. Edward Corwin argued in 1940 that the presidency had outgrown or exceeded its traditional constitutional limits and in fact was too powerful. By many accounts, presidential power has grown even more dramatically since then. Writing in 1973, Arthur M. Schlesinger Jr. decried what he said had become "The Imperial Presidency" (1973), especially in terms of presidential war powers. Dozens of other authors have criticized the presidential aggrandizement of power in recent decades, and many of them would view the unitary executive theory as just one aspect of that long-standing trend.

Compared to Other Theories of Executive Power

The unitary executive theory as such is unique to the United States, but it is broadly similar to several other theoretical accounts of executive power. In the English tradition, it is arguably related to John Locke's arguments in the *Second Treatise of Government* (1689) about the relation between executive and federative power, as well as Locke's discussion of executive prerogative, according to which the executive in a constitutional system may undertake actions that are not provided for by law, or that even go against the law, if they are done for the greater good.

It is also perhaps related to William Blackstone's account in his *Commentaries on the Laws of England* (1765–1769) of the division between executive and legislative power and his characterization that "the supreme executive power ... is vested ... in a single person," namely the monarch. In strikingly unitarian language, Blackstone said of executive power in the British constitution,

> This is wisely placed in a single hand by the British constitution, for the sake of unanimity, strength and dispatch. Were it placed in many hands, it would be subject to many wills: many wills, if disunited and drawing different ways, create weakness in a government: and to unite those several wills, and reduce them to one, is a work of more time and delay than the exigencies of state will afford.

In the French liberal tradition, unitarians are apt to note that Baron de Montesquieu argued in *The Spirit of the Laws* (1748) that the executive power should include foreign policy and that a single executive was best situated to execute the laws with dispatch. But in *The Principles of Politics Applicable to All Governments* (1810), Benjamin Constant argued for separating the power of the monarch from the power of the executive, to separate the execution of the law from the granting of pardons, contrary to a single or unitary executive.

In the twentieth century, Harvey Mansfield's provocative analysis of executive power in *Taming the Prince* (1989) has much to appeal to unitarians, especially his argument that executive power is impossible to limit or fully domesticate. However, his claim that executive is inherently tyrannical is more likely to appeal to critics of the unitary executive.

While the unitary executive theory may be compared with these and other well-known accounts of executive power, it is unique to the American context, as it is tied exclusively to the U.S. president and his constitutional powers.

The Founders

For unitarians, the theory of the unitary executive was a product of America's founding experience. Unitarians tend to point to the frustrations with the inadequate provisions for a national executive under the Articles of Confederation and also with the plural executives or governors that many of the states initially had, which were often themselves assisted by councils, thus further diluting the executive. According to Steven Calabresi and Christopher Yoo (2008, 33),

> by the time the framers gathered in Philadelphia on May 25, 1787 to revise the Articles of Confederation, the general antipathy toward executive power that dominated the post-1776 period immediately following independence had given way to a 1787 consensus in favor of an executive that was far more independent and energetic. Indeed, Madison listed the need 'to write a proper energy in the executive' as one of 'the great objects' of the Constitutional Convention.'

And as Hamilton later argued in *Federalist* 70, "The ingredients which constitute energy in the Executive are, first, unity ..."

Delegates at the Philadelphia convention debated how to structure the executive over several days in early June, 1787. Some (e.g., Elbridge Gerry, George Mason, and Edmund Randolph) favored a plural executive or a council, while others favored a single (or unitary) executive. James Wilson argued, "*Unity* in the Executive ... would be the best safeguard against tyranny." Ultimately, the delegates voted 7 to 3 in favor of a single executive (Orentlicher 2013, 145), perhaps because most assumed that George Washington would be the president and that he could be trusted to act responsibly and even to establish good precedents that would bind later presidents.

The Constitution

Most of the Constitution's treatment of the presidency is contained in Article II, which is just over 1,000 words long, and much of it is devoted to the procedure for presidential elections. The Constitution's treatment of presidential power is therefore quite brief, and it is also rather vague. The Constitution gives the president some formal powers and mentions executive departments, but it does not detail the president's relationship with the executive branch. Nevertheless, unitarians claim that the Constitution gives all executive power to the president.

Unitarians place particular importance on the "vesting clause" of Article II, which begins with the statement, "The executive Power shall be vested in a President of the United States of America." As Hamilton and others have noted, this stands in contrast to Article I's more limited conferral of legislative power to Congress: "All legislative powers herein granted shall be vested in a Congress of the United States." Since the qualifying term "herein granted" does not appear in Article II's grant of executive power, perhaps the Constitution embraces absolutely all power that is executive in nature and confers it entirely to just one person, with no portion reserved, shared, or allotted elsewhere. Additionally, unitarians often claim that the various specific powers mentioned in Article II are intended to be illustrative examples rather than a complete list, such that the president's grant of executive authority is general and includes many powers in addition to those that are mentioned.

Some unitarians also contend that the Constitution's directive that the president "shall take care that the laws be faithfully executed" makes sense only if he is vested with the executive power in general, as a less fulsome allotment of executive power would limit his ability to carry out the laws. Furthermore, some unitarians say that the president's oath "to execute the office of the President" and to "preserve, protect, and defend the Constitution" also indicates that the Constitution confers upon the president broad authority beyond what the text lists.

Benefits

Proponents of the unitary executive make various arguments about its alleged benefits. They claim that it accurately reflects the intentions of the American founders, especially Hamilton. They also argue that it is faithful to the constitutional text. As such, some argue, the unitary executive theory represents not just one possible understanding of the executive but rather the one that was intended and provided for, so that other conceptions are inauthentic or unconstitutional.

Unitarians also claim that the doctrine has a number of pragmatic benefits. They maintain that it is conducive to democratic governance, in that it avoids problems of collective action and unrepresentative or narrow interests. They also claim that it is good for effective administration, as it creates a clear chain of command and permits uniform application of the law. And they claim that it fosters political accountability, as it makes the president solely responsible for what the executive branch does and thus permits voters to hold him accountable by registering their (dis)approval of the performance of the executive branch.

Specific Issues

The different versions of the unitary executive theory naturally have different implications for what exactly a president may do in its name. But the theory is closely tied to several recurring controversies about presidential powers. In terms of specific issues, the unitary executive theory often comes up in disputes about the president's power to structure the bureaucracy, by changing the various entities within the executive branch. The theory also comes up in controversies about the president's ability to control, influence, or remove people within the executive branch.

Beyond executive structure and personnel, the unitary executive theory often factors into debates about the president issuing signing statements that express his judgment about the constitutionality of the legislation he signs into law, or that indicate his attitude toward the future implementation and enforcement of the law. Another recurring controversy in which the unitary executive theory often plays a role is the ability of the president to control the flow of information, often in relation to congressional requests for information, which the president may resist via the principle of executive privilege. And the unitary executive can be part of presidential claims about powers that are arguably discretionary or inherent. Insofar as the unitary executive theory is an element in issues like these, it is often part of major controversies about executive power.

Plan of the Book

This chapter has briefly introduced the theory of the unitary executive, including its basic elements, how it differs from other conceptions of the presidency, its theoretical relatives, its relevance to the founding era, its place in the Constitution, its alleged benefits, and the specific issues with which it tends to play a role. Building on this introduction, the following three chapters add some real details to those largely theoretical considerations by discussing how the unitary executive has developed historically.

Chapter 1 reviews the development of what would now be called the unitary executive from George Washington through Jimmy Carter. This period predates the explicit unitary executive theory, but there are numerous instances of early presidents acting much as modern unitarians would advocate. Chapter 2 discusses the unitary executive in the 1980s and 1990s, from its rise as an explicit doctrine under Ronald Reagan to its less prominent status under his two late-twentieth century successors. Chapter 3 examines the unitary executive in the twenty-first century: its return to prominence and indeed even greater controversy under George W. Bush, its less visible status under Barack Obama, and its apparent revival under Donald Trump.

After that historical analysis, Chapter 4 assesses some of the main normative arguments in favor of the unitary executive, including its alleged fidelity to the intentions of the founders and the constitutional text and its benefits for democratic governance, administrative efficiency, and accountability. Chapter 5 examines the empirical evidence for the unitary executive, or the extent to which the theory accurately describes reality. The concluding chapter argues that the unitary executive is a fundamentally political phenomenon, in several respects.

Conclusion

This book is intended to provide an accessible, evenhanded overview of the unitary executive theory and to demonstrate why it is important. Much of what follows is a synthesis of existing scholarly, journalistic, and governmental accounts, though rendered, combined, and updated per the author's own understanding. Readers who desire more detail or nuance may wish to consult the nearly 200 items in the bibliography for additional information. But for many readers, this book should serve to explain what the unitary executive theory is, why it matters, and whether it merits support or suspicion.

1
NEARLY TWO CENTURIES OF UNITARY PRECEDENTS

Although the theory of the unitary executive as such was not explicitly named or consciously promoted until the 1980s, there were many earlier precedents that some observers claim reflect a commitment to what would now be called the unitary executive. Indeed, in defending the theory of the unitary executive, Steven Calabresi and Christopher Yoo claimed in their book *The Unitary Executive: Presidential Power from Washington to Bush* (2008, 4) that "all of our nation's presidents have believed in the theory of the unitary executive." In their telling, even William Henry Harrison, who served as president for only one month and was a member of the Whig Party ideologically opposed to a strong executive, demonstrated support for robust presidential removal and appointment powers.

Strictly speaking, the claim that presidents before the late twentieth century supported the unitary executive is anachronistic, as it seeks to establish that something which was not named or fully described until the 1980s actually existed generations earlier. But the claim is nevertheless important for two reasons. First, insofar as it establishes that the unitary executive did not emerge from nothing in the Reagan years but rather built upon older precedents, it suggests that the unitary executive is not radically at odds with American political traditions.

Second, the Supreme Court has indicated that a long record of historical practices may inform constitutional understandings and to an extent even constitute constitutional arrangements. The classic statement on the importance of historical practice to the interpretation of presidential power is in Justice Felix Frankfurter's concurring opinion in *Youngstown Sheet & Tube Co. v. Sawyer* (1952):

> [A] systematic, unbroken, executive practice, long pursued to the knowledge of the Congress and never before questioned, engaged in by Presidents who have also sworn to uphold the Constitution, making as it were such exercise of power part of the structure of our government, may be treated as a gloss on "executive Power" vested in the President by § 1 of Art. II.

Thus, if there were voluminous evidence of a proto-unitary executive and congressional acquiescence to it before the 1980s, then the doctrine might be constitutional.

This chapter examines episodes concerning what would later be called the unitary executive from George Washington through the 1970s, or nearly the country's first two centuries. The aim is to explore how some of the theoretical concerns noted in the previous chapter have played out in the real world of interbranch politics, and also to lay the historical foundation for the discussion in the next two chapters of the more direct and dramatic invocations of the unitary executive theory in more recent decades.

The Eighteenth Century

On some interpretations, the unitary executive dates to the earliest days of the republic. In what was essentially the first executive order ever issued by a president, in 1789 George Washington ordered holdover officials from the old government of the Articles of Confederation "to impress me with a full, precise, and distinct general idea of the affairs of the United States" with which they dealt. The effort to control the activities of subordinates is a key part of the unitary executive, and Washington's order arguably reflected that sensibility.

Also, in 1789, the very first Congress debated the creation of cabinet departments within the executive branch, each to be headed by a Secretary, who would be removable by the president. But concern soon arose about the nature of the president's removal power, which is a prime feature of the unitary executive. Members of Congress disagreed about whether the president already had the power to remove such officials based on the language of Article II (i.e., the unitarian interpretation), or Congress would have to delegate a removal power to the president, or any removal would require the consent of the Senate, or if impeachment was the only legitimate way to remove an official. Congress debated the issue for over a month and finally passed bills to create the Departments of Foreign Affairs, Treasury, and War, without explicitly giving the president a removal power for those officials. For today's unitarians, this indicated that Congress believed the president already possessed the removal power via the Constitution. Indeed, as George W. Bush's Deputy Assistant Attorney General John Yoo wrote in an Office of Legal Counsel (OLC) opinion over 200 years later, "As reflected in the great debate over removal in the very first Congress, the Framers rejected a legislative role in removal in favor of plenary presidential power over officers appointed by the President …"

John Adams's presidency was marked by intolerance of political dissent, and that attitude extended to his own Cabinet. In 1800, Adams asked for Secretary of War James McHenry to resign, and he also dismissed Secretary of State Timothy Pickering, after they opposed Adams's policy of making peace with France. Again, a president's ability to control and remove subordinates is key to the unitary executive.

The Nineteenth Century

Thomas Jefferson initiated several actions that were in keeping with the unitary executive. He ordered Secretary of State James Madison to withhold the commissions for several of John Adams's "midnight" judicial appointments that Adams's Secretary of State, John Marshall, had failed to deliver before the end of Adams's term, including that of would-be justice of the peace William Marbury. The controversy soon led to the case of *Marbury v. Madison* (1803), in which Marshall, who was then the Chief Justice, ruled that the Court could not compel the executive branch to deliver Marbury's commission. Jefferson's other quasi-unitarian actions included his nonenforcement of the Sedition Act of 1798, which he thought was unconstitutional, and granting pardon for people who had been convicted of violating it. In 1803, Jefferson initiated the Louisiana Purchase, even though he believed that the Constitution gave him no authority to do so. Unitarians tend to support that sort of bold presidentialism, even if it is not explicitly provided for by the Constitution. Jefferson also arguably exhibited the unitarian practice of directing subordinates to follow the president's desires rather than those of another branch, as he instructed revenue collectors to hold a vessel in order to enforce a trade embargo, and he ordered them to ignore judicial decisions that he lacked such authority (Yoo 2010, 246 n19).

In 1822, James Monroe issued what might now be called presidential signing statements, as he sent two messages to Congress to express concerns about the constitutionality of a statute which he felt wrongly limited his power to make certain military appointments. Monroe complained that the law amounted to "taking from the President all agency in their appointment" and that "Such a construction would not only be subversive of the obvious principles of the Constitution, but utterly inconsistent with the spirit of the law itself."

In the 1830s, Andrew Jackson undertook several unitarian actions. He refused to enforce the Supreme Court's decision in *Worcester v. Georgia* (1832), which favored Cherokee control over tribal lands in Georgia. Jackson allegedly declared "John Marshall has made his decision, now let him enforce it," and although the quotation might be apocryphal, the president's refusal to accept the constitutional determination of the judiciary was clear.

One year later, Jackson sought to remove federal funds from the Second Bank of the United States, which he opposed. Treasury Secretary Louis McLane refused to remove government deposits from the bank, so Jackson replaced him with William Duane. When Duane also refused to remove the deposits, Jackson fired him. When the Senate asked Jackson to provide documents relating to his opposition to the bank, he refused to comply. This led the Senate to censure Jackson in March 1834, for assuming "authority and power not conferred by the Constitution." (Several years later his censure was expunged.) In his message to the Senate of April 15, 1834 to protest his censure, Jackson explained his view of presidential purview over personnel:

> The whole executive power being vested in the President, who is responsible for its exercise, it is a necessary consequence that he should have a right to employ agents of his own choice to aid him in the performance of his duties, and to discharge them when he is no longer willing to be responsible for their acts. In strict accordance with this principle, the power of removal, which like that of appointment, is an original executive power, is left unchecked by the Constitution in relation to all executive officers.

In 1835, Jackson's new Postmaster General Amos Kendall refused to honor a contract that his predecessor had made. When the District of Columbia circuit court ordered him to honor it, he refused. And when Congress passed a law in 1836 instructing him to honor it, he still refused. Kendall argued that the law infringed upon an area of executive control and that the contracts were based on political favoritism. In *Kendall v. the United States*

(1838), the Court said that Congress or the courts can order executive officials to perform statutorily required ministerial duties, but that such control does not extend to duties that involve executive discretion. In short, the Court said some executive branch actions were subject to the control of the other branches, while other actions were not:

> There are certain political duties imposed upon many officers in the executive department the discharge of which is under the direction of the President. But it would be an alarming doctrine that Congress cannot impose upon any executive officer any duty they may think proper which is not repugnant to any rights secured and protected by the Constitution, and, in such cases, the duty and responsibility grow out of and are subject to the control of the law, and not to the direction of the President. And this is emphatically the case where the duty enjoined is of a mere ministerial character.

The Court felt that Kendall's actions fell into the ministerial category and therefore said that he had to do what Congress had ordered.

However, regarding the argument that the President could supposedly direct the postmaster general because of the "take care" clause, the Court said:

> This doctrine cannot receive the sanction of this court. It would be vesting in the President a dispensing power which has no countenance for its support in any part of the Constitution, and is asserting a principle, which, if carried out in its results to all cases falling within it, would be clothing the President with a power entirely to control the legislation of Congress and paralyze the administration of justice.

Abraham Lincoln claimed emergency powers in 1861 to fight the Civil War, a claim that most unitarians would accept. However, he did not claim that his actions were constitutional, as most unitarians would, and he later wrote to Congress to defend his actions. Lincoln also ignored Chief Justice Roger Taney's ruling in *Ex parte Merryman* (1861) against the president's right to suspend the writ of habeas corpus. Lincoln criticized Taney's decision in an address to Congress, and he continued to suspend the writ as he saw fit, refusing to accept the Court's determination of what was constitutional.

After Lincoln was assassinated, Andrew Johnson sparred with Radical Republicans in Congress over Reconstruction and even faced opposition from his own Cabinet, particularly Secretary of War Edwin Stanton.

Johnson tried repeatedly to remove Stanton, even after Congress passed the 1867 Tenure of Office Act over his veto to limit the president's removal power by requiring senatorial approval. Johnson believed that the Tenure of Office Act was unconstitutional, and he tried to appoint a new Secretary of War in part to challenge the law in court. This led to his impeachment in February 1868.

The last several decades of the nineteenth century are often regarded as a period of congressional dominance, in which Congress asserted itself while presidents seldom did so, and that basic dynamic can be seen in issues relevant to the unitary executive. For example, the Interstate Commerce Act of 1887 led to the creation of the Interstate Commerce Commission (ICC), which was arguably the first independent agency. Future presidents would strongly oppose independent entities within the bureaucracy, per the unitarian view that the chief executive must control the entire executive branch.

Other aspects of this era suggest a more nuanced dynamic with regard to the unitary executive. For example, the Pendleton Civil Service Act of 1883 shifted federal employment from political spoils to a merit-based system and made it illegal to fire employees for political reasons, but it did not otherwise reduce the president's power to manage or remove employees. And when congressional Republicans sought to limit the president's ability to remove officials in 1887, Grover Cleveland fought back and successfully insisted on the repeal of the Tenure of Office Act, which he saw as an unconstitutional infringement on the president's power of removal.

The Twentieth Century

In 1899, William McKinley issued an order to remove a government appraiser, who then refused to leave his job and continued to work without being paid. This led to the case of *Shurtleff v. United States* (1903), in which the Supreme Court upheld McKinley's right to remove the official. Relying on several earlier cases, the Court endorsed a robust presidential removal power:

> it cannot be doubted that, in the absence of constitutional or statutory provision, the President can, by virtue of his general power of appointment, remove an officer, even though appointed by and with the advice and consent of the Senate.

If McKinley presaged a return to a more assertive presidency, Theodore Roosevelt (TR) made it clear that Congress and the courts would have to deal with a powerful and active president. TR articulated the "stewardship" theory of presidential leadership, claiming that the president was uniquely able to discern the national interest and to advance it. Indeed, TR believed that the president should be at the forefront of an activist federal government. And he coupled this view of the primacy of the presidency with an expansive view of presidential power, according to which the president could act as he saw fit unless explicitly forbidden from doing so; for TR the Constitution limited rather than empowered the president. TR explained these points in his autobiography (1913):

> My view was that every executive officer, and above all every executive officer in high position, was a steward of the people bound actively and affirmatively to do all he could for the people, and not to content himself with the negative merit of keeping his talents undamaged in a napkin. I declined to adopt the view that what was imperatively necessary for the Nation could not be done by the President unless he could find some specific authorization to do it. My belief was that it was not only his right but his duty to do anything that the needs of the Nation demanded unless such action was forbidden by the Constitution or by the laws. Under this interpretation of executive power I did and caused to be done many things not previously done by the President and the heads of the departments. I did not usurp power, but I did greatly broaden the use of executive power. In other words, I acted for the public welfare, I acted for the common well-being of all our people, whenever and in whatever manner was necessary, unless prevented by direct constitutional or legislative prohibition.

Driven by these principles, TR issued a great many executive orders and proclamations to advance Progressive causes, despite opposition from various quarters. For example, in 1904 he ordered the redesign of U.S. coins, contrary to the wishes of the U.S. Mint. In 1905, without consulting Congress, he issued an executive order to create the Committee on Department Methods, better known as the Keep Commission, and directed it to study administrative reforms. Congress perceived this as a presidential effort to seize control of the bureaucracy, so it ignored the committee's recommendations, it refused to appropriate funds to publish the recommendations, and it passed a law forbidding the future creation of commissions by executive order. TR also used executive orders to enact controversial changes concerning the civil service, work conditions and union efforts for government employees, and veterans' pensions, among other issues.

Although TR's successor William Howard Taft adhered to a more limited view of presidential power, Woodrow Wilson was more active. As a scholar, Wilson had favored keeping administration independent from political influence. But as president, Wilson oversaw the segregation of federal offices, he issued an executive order to suspend the eight-hour workday for government employees, he secured passage of a law that permitted him to reorganize parts of the government, and he issued an executive order to create the War Industries Board to coordinate production efforts for World War I.

In 1920, Wilson ordered the removal of postmaster Frank Myers, contrary to a law from 1876 that called for the Senate to consent to any removal of postmasters. In *Myers v. United States* (1926), the Court voted 5-4 to uphold the president's exclusive power to remove executive branch officials. Chief Justice (and former President) Taft wrote the majority opinion, in which he articulated a robust defense of the president's removal power. Taft drew on the *Decision of 1789* and argued that Congress could not place any restrictions on the president's ability to remove an executive official.

Unitarians tend to cite *Myers* as defending a broad presidential power to remove subordinates, but Taft's opinion did note some areas in which a president's power to control, change, or influence executive officials' determinations was limited, even if the president's power to fire the officials was not:

> Of course, there may be duties so peculiarly and specifically committed to the discretion of a particular officer as to raise a question whether the President may overrule or revise the officer's interpretation of his statutory duty in a particular instance. Then there may be duties of a *quasi*-judicial character imposed on executive officers and members of executive tribunals whose decisions after hearing affect interests of individuals, the discharge of which the President cannot in a particular case properly influence or control. But even in such a case, he may consider the decision after its rendition as a reason for removing the officer, on the ground that the discretion regularly entrusted to that officer by statute has not been, on the whole, intelligently or wisely exercised. Otherwise, he does not discharge his own constitutional duty of seeing that the laws be faithfully executed.

Taft viewed the case as a landmark and was disappointed that not all of the justices supported his interpretation. Nevertheless, three justices issued dissenting opinions in *Myers*, one of which, by Justice James Clark McReynolds, was 62 pages long and denounced Taft's view as "revolutionary." (As it turned out, Taft's view would prevail for less than a decade.)

Franklin Delano Roosevelt

Franklin Roosevelt is generally regarded as the father of the modern presidency, and his remarkable 12 years in office included not just extraordinary actions to address the Great Depression and World War II, but also actions that touched on the themes of the unitary executive. In 1933, FDR sought to remove a holdover Hoover official, William Humphrey, from the Federal Trade Commission (FTC), because of differences of opinion about policy. When Humphrey refused to resign, FDR fired him, in apparent violation of the 1914 Federal Trade Act, which provided for the presidential removal of a commissioner only for "inefficiency, neglect of duty, or malfeasance."

In *Humphrey's Executor v. United States* (1935), the Court unanimously found that FDR was wrong to fire Humphrey. The Court made a distinction between administrative officials who had executive powers and those who had duties that were in some sense judicial or legislative. For the latter group, it said that Congress could place limits on the president's power of removal. Thus, *Humphrey's* rejected the expansive presidential removal power of *Myers*. More broadly, by recognizing that some executive branch officials had nonexecutive functions, the case facilitated the growth of independent entities within the executive branch.

Proponents of the unitary executive see *Humphrey's* as being incorrectly decided, but they are far more favorably disposed to a case that came a year later, *United States v. Curtiss-Wright Export Corp.* (1936). The case concerned an arms embargo that FDR proclaimed, after Congress authorized him to do so. The Court found that the president possessed broad independent constitutional powers in the realm of foreign affairs. As Justice George Sutherland wrote:

> we are here dealing not alone with an authority vested in the President by an exertion of legislative power, but with such an authority plus the very delicate, plenary and exclusive power of the President as the sole organ of the federal government in the field of international relations – a power which does not require as a basis for its exercise an act of Congress.

Sutherland's characterization of the president's power in foreign relations drew on a congressional speech that John Marshall had given in 1800 in the House of Representatives, a year before he became Chief Justice. The assertion of an exclusive and inherent presidential power over foreign affairs has appealed to many unitarians ever since.

Despite the setback of *Humphrey's*, FDR still sought to control the federal bureaucracy, including independent agencies. In 1936, FDR created a committee to assess the organization of the executive branch and its administrative management. In 1937, the President's Committee on Administrative Management, better known as the Brownlow Committee, declared "The President needs help." It recommended major changes to the executive branch, including presidential control of departments. The Brownlow Committee was particularly concerned about the president's (in)ability to control independent agencies, which it referred to as a "headless fourth branch of government:"

> The independent commissions present a serious immediate problem. No administrative reorganization worthy of the name can leave hanging in the air more than a dozen powerful, irresponsible agencies free to determine policy and administer law. Any program to restore our constitutional ideal of a fully coordinated Executive Branch responsible to the President must bring within the reach of that responsible control all work done by these independent commissions which is not judicial in nature. That challenge cannot be ignored.

FDR supported the Brownlow Committee's recommendations, particularly its call to abolish independent agencies, but in 1938 Congress rejected its recommendations.

In 1939, however, Congress acceded to requests to improve executive administration, as it passed legislation that created the Executive Office of the President (EOP), consolidated 105 agencies into 12 departments, created an auditor general to monitor expenditures, and gave the president authority to appoint six assistants and to submit plans for reorganizing departments to Congress. Many scholars trace the modern presidency to the creation of the EOP, as it greatly facilitated the president's administrative authority. Furthermore, as part of the 1939 reorganization, FDR moved the Bureau of the Budget to the EOP to better coordinate departmental initiatives, a change that would facilitate greater presidential control.

The Mid-Twentieth Century

Harry Truman's sympathy with certain unitarian aims was suggested by the sign on his Oval Office desk which read, "The buck stops here," indicating that the president is ultimately in charge. Yet, Truman once complained, "I thought I was the president, but when it comes to these bureaucrats, I can't do a damn thing" (Nathan 1983, 1). In terms of quasi-unitarian actions, Truman initially resisted Congress's creation of the National Security Council (NSC) in 1947, as he disliked Congress dictating who could advise him. He attended its first meeting but then distanced himself from its activities and sought national security advice elsewhere.

Truman asserted inherent power in 1950 by going to war in Korea without a formal declaration of war from Congress. He also invoked the idea of inherent power regarding his seizure of most of the nation's steel mills in 1952. Ten days after oral arguments at the Supreme Court about the steel seizure, Truman's secretary gave a reporter an official addendum to remarks the president had made about the case at a press conference:

> Neither the Congress nor the courts could deny the inherent powers of the Presidency without tearing up the Constitution. The President said that the Supreme Court, in the pending steel case, might properly decide that the conditions existing did not justify the use by the President of his inherent powers, but that such a decision would not deny the existence of the inherent powers.

Eleven days later, the Court overturned Truman's action in *Youngstown Sheet & Tube Co. v. Sawyer.* Justice Robert Jackson's concurring opinion described how presidential and congressional power can overlap and said that presidential authority to act was greatest when Congress approves of it.

In Dwight Eisenhower's presidency, the Court once again considered the president's removal power, in the case of *Wiener v. United States* (1958). The Court ruled unanimously that Eisenhower was wrong to have fired a member of the War Claims Commission who had served under Truman just because Eisenhower wanted to replace him with his own appointee. Quoting *Humphrey's*, the Court said the commission was an independent federal agency that was supposed to be "entirely free from the control or coercive influence" of either the president or Congress. Regarding "the claim that the President could remove a member of an adjudicatory body like the War Claims Commission merely because he wanted his own appointees on such a Commission," the Court said,

> we are compelled to conclude that no such power is given to the President directly by the Constitution, and none is impliedly conferred upon him by statute simply because Congress said nothing about it. The philosophy of *Humphrey's Executor*, in its explicit language as well as its implications, precludes such a claim.

During Lyndon Johnson's presidency, cost-benefit analysis began for the Army Corps of Engineers and soon spread to other areas through the Bureau of the Budget. Some see this as the beginning of centralized regulatory review, a practice that expanded significantly later in the twentieth century. LBJ also created various task forces to help organize policy initiatives, including a Task Force on Government Organization. And LBJ's Executive Order 11,315 of 1966 created a new group of federal positions called Noncareer Executive Assignments that were outside the civil service, facilitating greater presidential influence in federal agencies.

Richard Nixon

Richard Nixon was a central figure in the development of what would become the unitary executive theory and in many respects was essentially a proto-unitarian. As David Alvis et al. (2013, 176) note, "the rise of the unitarians had an important precursor in the events that unfolded under Richard Nixon's presidency." Similarly, Stephen Skowronek (2009, 2098) says, "The Nixon Administration anticipated at a practical level what the new theory would soon seek to elevate as a standard rule." More specifically, Nixon is seen as the creator of the "administrative presidency," via which the president would do administratively what he could not do legislatively. In 1975, Richard Nathan termed Nixon's efforts in to govern via managing as "the plot that failed," but subsequent developments suggest that it did not altogether fail.

As if to physically mark his determination to control the executive branch, Nixon maintained his principle office not in the White House but in room 108 of the Old Executive Office Building (OEOB), which housed many high-level executive branch officials and entities. Other presidents had occasionally used space there, but Nixon used it as his main work location, with the Oval Office relegated mostly to ceremonial functions. (Indeed, some of the tape recordings of Nixon's conversations relating to the Watergate scandal were made in his OEOB office.)

Shortly after his election in 1968, Nixon created the President's Advisory Council on Executive Organization, better known as the Ash Council, after its head Robert Ash. Over the next three years, the council issued 13 memos to the president with various suggestions for administrative reforms. One suggested reform was to establish a Domestic Council within the EOP, which Nixon did by executive order in March 1970. Modeled on the National Security Council (NSC), the Domestic Council would facilitate presidential control of domestic policymaking and was led by John Ehrlichman.

The Ash Council also recommended changing the Bureau of the Budget into a new Office of Executive Management, an entity that became the new Office of Management and Budget (OMB), which Nixon created by Executive Order 11,541 in July 1970. OMB was to help the president coordinate policy and monitor the executive branch. Ash himself became the head of OMB in 1973. OMB's oversight soon grew from just EPA regulations to include "quality of life" (QOL) review of various draft regulations. By some accounts, this created the first program for presidential review of the regulatory process. Subsequent presidents greatly expanded it. As Alvis et al. (2013, 182) explain, Congress resisted this:

> Congress did not sit by idly as Nixon concentrated power in the executive branch. Most notably, Congress attempted to remove Nixon's OMB director and the deputy OMB director by abolishing their positions and then reestablishing them subject to Senate confirmation. The congressional bill led to an early showdown over executive power between Nixon and Congress ... Nixon vetoed the bill in May 1973 because "the power of the Congress to terminate an office cannot be used as a back-door method of circumventing the president's power to remove."

Persuaded by another recommendation of the Ash Council, in 1971 Nixon sought congressional authorization to restructure executive departments by combining seven existing departments into four new and larger ones. When Congress declined to authorize such a change, Nixon sought to do it unilaterally in 1973, by assigning "super-secretaries" to coordinate the departments as if they had been officially combined in the way that he wanted.

Nixon's presidency was marked by controversies over impoundment, whereby the president decides to spend less than the amount that Congress had appropriated and the president had signed into law. Previous presidents had impounded funds, but Nixon did so aggressively and routinely, in some years impounding 20% of the funds he could control that had been appropriated by Congress. As with many unitary executive controversies, the debate was whether the president possessed this power via Article II or if it was instead a power delegated by Congress and therefore subject to its approval. Nixon claimed the former, as in 1973 he asserted, "The constitutional right for the President of the United States to impound funds ... is absolutely clear." One year later, the Budget and Impoundment Act banned the practice of impoundment.

On October 20, 1973, Nixon's "Saturday Night Massacre" dramatically highlighted the controversy over the president's removal power. Nixon ordered Attorney General Elliott Richardson to fire Watergate special prosecutor Archibald Cox, who had been on the job for five months and had pushed for Nixon to release secret tape recordings, which Nixon refused to do despite an order from a federal appeals court, citing executive privilege. Richardson refused to fire Cox and instead resigned himself in protest. Nixon then ordered Deputy Attorney General William Ruckelshaus to fire Cox, but he also refused and resigned. Undeterred, Nixon tried for a third time and managed to get Solicitor General Robert Bork to fire Cox. Bork acceded to Nixon's request in part because he believed it would exacerbate the crisis if no official would carry out the president's order.

While actions like those noted above suggest clear affinities between Nixon and the unitary executive, it is some of Nixon's rhetoric that is perhaps most strikingly unitarian. The following well-known exchange from Nixon's 1977 interview with the journalist David Frost is instructive:

NIXON: "Well, when the president does it, that means that it is not illegal."
FROST: "By definition."
NIXON: "Exactly. Exactly."

Nixon thus suggested that a presidential act cannot be illegal. Furthermore, Nixon's next comments to Frost indicated that the president's alleged immunity to illegality could also cover his subordinates:

If the president, for example, approves something because of the national security, or in this case because of a threat to internal peace and order of significant magnitude, then the president's decision in that instance is one that enables those who carry it out, to carry it out without violating a law.

The 1970s

Following Nixon's remarkable five and one-half years in office, historical analysis of unitary or forceful presidential actions tends to turn to the 1980s and to gloss over the rest of the 1970s. Gerald Ford and Jimmy Carter had to deal with a resurgent Congress, but both presidents exhibited some unitarian traits. For example, both used presidential signing statements to express concerns or to indicate how they would implement laws. Both resisted the limits of the 1973 War Powers Act. And both also expanded OMB's oversight. Ford issued Executive Order 11,821 in 1974 to direct the Council on Wage and Price Stability to evaluate the inflationary impact of proposed regulations. And in 1978 Carter issued Executive Order 12,044 to direct agencies to write regulatory impact analyses and also created new oversight groups to monitor compliance with his regulatory procedure. Carter wanted to extend regulatory review to independent agencies but relented because of concerns about the legitimate reach of executive authority.

The last couple years of Carter's presidency saw several developments that would become major flash points for the unitary executive under later presidents. First, in October 1978 Congress passed the Civil Service Reform Act regarding the dismissal of federal employees, and it created the Senior Executive Service (SES), which permitted the president to make numerous political appointments to departments and agencies. Second, the Ethics in Government Act (EIGA) of 1978, which responded to the view that the executive branch could not be trusted to investigate itself, permitted the creation of an independent special prosecutor, a position that later became known as an independent counsel. This was anathema to proponents of what would soon become the unitary executive. Third, OMB's Office of Regulatory Affairs (OIRA) was established by Congress in December 1980 to monitor the Paperwork Reduction Act, but it would soon see far greater use under Reagan for controlling regulations.

Conclusion

This chapter has briefly surveyed some of the major actions and controversies related to what would later be called the unitary executive theory from George Washington through Jimmy Carter. We saw conflicts regarding the president's removal power, directing subordinates, control of the bureaucracy and regulation, assuming powers not in the Constitution, and other matters. Some of the episodes discussed here are deeply historical and might seem to be of limited relevance for more recent events, but some of these early precedents are very important and greatly influenced events during the last four decades, as the next two chapters will demonstrate.

2
EXPLICIT UNITARY BATTLES IN THE 1980s AND 1990s

Although there were numerous presidential actions during the nation's first two centuries that in one way or another accorded with what would later be called the theory of the unitary executive, it was not until the 1980s that the unitary executive really rose to prominence. This is because it was during Ronald Reagan's presidency that the term "unitary executive" was first explicitly employed and the theory was first promoted. Earlier presidents might have sometimes acted as proto-unitarians, but Reagan was the first to consciously use and advocate the doctrine.

Whereas the previous chapter covered nearly two centuries and dozens of presidents, this chapter covers just two decades and three presidents, namely Ronald Reagan and his two late-twentieth century successors. The aim is to examine how and why the doctrine of the unitary executive was initiated and promulgated under Reagan and whether or to what extent it was institutionalized such that it outlasted the particular circumstances of his presidency and was also utilized by his immediate successors.

Ronald Reagan

The genesis of the explicit unitary executive theory under Reagan is important because the conception was not uncovered in the course of some disinterested academic research about constitutional origins, legal developments, or historical precedents. It was consciously created and deployed for overtly political purposes, specifically to assist a decidedly conservative president's efforts to significantly change political commitments that had dominated American politics since the days of the New Deal. The theory of the unitary executive came into being in order to provide an ostensibly principled rationale and justification for conservatives to stop and reverse the growth of government; it was rooted in and motivated by politics, not the Constitution.

For students of American political history, there is an irony to conservatives promulgating a rationale for presidential prominence. For most of the twentieth century, it had been progressives who called for a more powerful president, while conservatives – "cuing off a hallowed Whig tradition of hostility to presidential aggrandizement and executive pretension" (Skowronek 2009, 2075) – had been inclined to favor the American constitutional order's various limits and checks as an effective barrier to governmental overreach. However, once they gained political power, some conservatives came to see such limits as an irritating barrier to executive action that could advance conservative ideals. Conservatives who had championed systematic constraints while progressives were in office chaffed at such inconveniences once they came to power. As Jeffrey Rosen explains, in the 1980s, conservatives "came to see a strong presidency as the only way to defend conservative ideals from the encroachments of a Democratic Congress, liberal courts, and obstreperous bureaucrats." In short, as Stephen Skowronek (2009, 2075) has noted, "The theory of the unitary executive promotes exactly what the earlier generation of conservatives feared." There is the additional irony that conservatives have often decried alleged governmental overreach or intrusion on the grounds that actions that are not explicitly provided for by the Constitution are inherently suspect and should not be creatively read into it, yet the unitary executive theory had been criticized on exactly those grounds.

Its politics and historical pedigree aside, the unitary executive was explicitly promoted in the 1980s by a cadre of people within the Reagan administration, especially the Office of Legal Counsel (OLC) and the Federalist Society of conservative lawyers. These included Edwin Meese, Steven Calabresi, Samuel Alito, Ted Olson, Charles Cooper, Michael Stokes Paulsen, and Douglas Kmiec, among others. They did not agree about everything, and some officials in the administration even opposed them. For example, as journalist Charlie Savage (2007, 45) has noted, Solicitor General Charles Fried thought that some of young lawyers whom Meese encouraged were too radical, as when they questioned the constitutionality of independent agencies or suggested that the president could ignore Court decisions. Nevertheless, the unitarians held considerable sway in the Reagan administration.

Reagan used the term "unitary executive" a half-dozen times during his eight years in office, and his administration undertook many actions that accorded with the theory.

The Removal Power

On the day of his inauguration, Reagan removed all 15 agency Inspectors General (IGs) who had been appointed by Carter. Created by the 1978 Inspector General Act, the IGs serve as internal watchdogs against corruption and waste in federal agencies. They occupy a difficult position between executive and legislative control, as they have to report to agency heads and also to Congress. When Congress complained that the removals would politicize the nonpartisan positions, Reagan rehired many of the fired IGs.

Regulatory Review

Four weeks after his inauguration, Reagan issued Executive Order 12,291 in an effort to reduce federal regulation and to put the president at the center of regulatory oversight. Indeed, one of the order's stated purposes was to "provide for presidential oversight of the regulatory process." Reagan's order required agencies to perform a cost-benefit analysis of regulations, to develop a regulatory impact analysis (RIA), and to submit their rules to OIRA for review. The order also instituted retrospective regulatory review.

In January 1985, at the end of his first term, Reagan issued Executive Order 12,498 to enhance the system of regulatory review he had established previously. It directed agencies to write annual regulatory reports, which would be reviewed by OMB. It also sought to facilitate prospective regulatory planning. And it said, "The head of each Executive agency subject to this Order shall ensure that all regulatory actions are consistent with the goals of the agency and of the Administration."

Signing Statements

Presidential signing statements were a key part of the unitary executive under Reagan. By some accounts (Rosen), Steven Calabresi came up with the idea of using signing statements to guard the president's constitutional powers. Samuel Alito also promoted the use of signing as a member of the Litigation Strategy Working Group. In 1986, he encouraged increased use of the practice but said it should be done slowly, to limit congressional resistance. In February 1986, Edwin Meese announced that a signing statement would be placed in the legislative history section of the *United States Code Congressional and Administrative News* (USCCAN), "to make sure that the President's own understanding of what's in a bill ... is given consideration ... later on by a court." In total, over one-third of Reagan's 250 signing statements articulated objections to statutory provisions. For example, his signing statement for the 1986 Fisheries Act said that Congress could not remove commissioners of the Great Lakes Fishery Commission. Reagan's signing statement of September 29, 1987 for a bill to increase the federal debt ceiling explicitly referenced the unitary executive: "If this provision were interpreted otherwise, so as to require the President to follow the orders of a subordinate, it would plainly constitute an unconstitutional infringement of the President's authority as head of a unitary executive branch."

Meese's Report

In April 1986, Attorney General Edwin Meese received an 80-page report on "Separation of Powers: Legislative-Executive Relations." Meese had commissioned the report from the Justice Department's Domestic Policy Committee, an internal "think tank" staffed with conservative scholars and policy advisers. The report did not use the term "unitary executive," but it was clearly driven by the theory. It argued for a radically strict separation of powers to prevent Congress from wrongly usurping executive authority. It also lauded Reagan's assertions of executive power, it noted various legislative encroachments on the executive branch (e.g., the 1973 War Powers Act), and it endorsed nonenforcement and signing statements as means of resisting such encroachments.

The Iran-Contra Scandal

Congress's reaction to the Iran-Contra scandal also touched on unitarian themes. The official report of the joint congressional committee found that the Reagan Administration had shown "disdain for the law" by using funds from secretly selling weapons to Iran, despite an arms embargo, to fund the Contras rebel groups battling the Sandinista government in Nicaragua, contrary to the Boland Amendment against funding the Contras. But the November 1987 congressional minority report came to a different conclusion. The minority report was signed by eight Members of Congress, apparently written by Michael Malbin and David Addington, and promoted by Dick Cheney (who was then a Representative from Wyoming). For Cheney and others, the problem was not that the Reagan administration had broken the law, but that Congress has passed such a law in the first place. The minority report claimed that Congress had wrongly sought to curtail the executive's ability to conduct foreign affairs. The report drew on Alexander Hamilton to offer a robust defense of broad executive power, in particular with regard to control of foreign policy:

> the President was expected to have the primary role of conducting the foreign policy of the United States. Congressional actions to limit the President in this area therefore should be reviewed with a considerable degree of skepticism. If they interfere with core presidential foreign policy functions, they should be struck down. Moreover, the lesson of our constitutional history is that doubtful cases should be decided in favor of the President.

AIDS Information

Another unitary issue for Reagan involved a dispute in 1988 with the Centers for Disease Control and Prevention (CDC) over the publication of a pamphlet with information about contracting HIV/AIDS and how to prevent it. Congress passed a law calling for the publication of such a pamphlet, but Reagan refused, partly because of conservatives' concerns about sexuality and morality. Congress then passed a statute directing the head of the CDC that such a pamphlet must be prepared and "distributed without necessary clearance of the content by any official, organization or office."

Reagan's Department of Justice complained that this was unconstitutional because it infringed on the president's ability to direct his subordinates. The OLC issued a memo which said that since the CDC was within the Department of Health and Human Service (HSS), the legislation "violates the separation of powers by unconstitutionally infringing upon the president's authority to supervise the executive branch." The memo said it "prevents the President, either directly or through his subordinates, from supervising a subordinate executive branch official … trenching upon the president's exclusive constitutional authority to supervise the executive branch." The memo explicitly invoked the unitary executive, declaring that "As the head of a unitary executive, the President controls all subordinate officials within the executive branch." It also said, "Any attempt by Congress to constrain the President's authority to supervise and direct his subordinates ... violates the Constitution." (Ultimately, an 8-page brochure on "Understanding AIDS" authored by Surgeon General C. Everett Koop was mailed to every American household. Members of the Domestic Policy Council asked to see it before it was sent out, but no changes were made.)

Court Cases

The Reagan administration resisted congressional efforts to control executive actions by a legislative veto. Since the 1930s, Congress had used this device on hundreds of occasions to control agencies to which it had delegated power by retaining the ability to object after the fact to how the agencies had carried out their tasks, contrary to the tenets of the unitary executive. The Immigration and Nationality Act permitted either the House or Senate to invalidate deportation rulings by the Attorney General. A would-be deportee argued that this was unconstitutional because it enabled the legislature to encroach upon an area of executive control. In *INS v. Chadha* (1983), the Court essentially found the practice of using a legislative veto to be unconstitutional. Chief Justice Warren Burger declared,

> the fact that a given law or procedure is efficient, convenient, and useful in facilitating functions of government, standing alone, will not save it if it is contrary to the Constitution. Convenience and efficiency are not the primary objectives ... or the hallmarks ... of democratic government.

In response, Attorney General William French Smith praised the Court, which he said had "reaffirmed in a strong and compelling opinion the vital and important role under our Constitution of the principle of separation of powers."

In July 1984, Reagan signed the Competition in Contracting Act (CICA) into law but issued a signing statement which declared that a portion of the bill was unconstitutional because it gave the Comptroller General too much independence. Attorney General Smith then issued an opinion that said the law was unconstitutional, and OMB ordered federal agencies to "take no action, including the issuance of regulations, based upon the invalid provisions." The administration refused to defend the law in a subsequent court case (*Ameron Inc. v. U.S. Army Corps of Engineers*, 1985), but a Third District judge upheld it and ruled that the administration had to follow the entirety of the law. Attorney General Edwin Meese claimed that the executive branch had inherent power to interpret the Constitution, and he declared that the administration would not obey the judge's ruling. The Tenth Circuit Court then upheld the ruling against the administration. In 1986, the Chairman of the House Judiciary Committee threatened to cut off funding for Meese's office unless the White House obeyed the court rulings, and ultimately Meese withdrew his objections and OMB cancelled its order (Kelley 2002, 8).

In 1986, the Reagan administration challenged the Comptroller General's position under the Gramm-Rudman-Hollings Act of 1985. The Comptroller General is an officer of Congress but under the act was essentially given authority to make decisions about the executive branch and was not subject to removal by the president. The DC district court held that the act violated the separation of powers. Antonin Scalia was on the 3-judge panel, and he used the occasion to deride the implication of *Humphrey's Executor* that there could be a "headless fourth branch," employing the phrase of the 1937 Brownlow Committee that equated independent agencies with a bureaucracy uncontrolled by the executive. The opinion complained, "It has ... always been difficult to reconcile *Humphrey's Executor's* 'headless fourth branch' with a constitutional text and tradition establishing three branches of government ..."

Two months later, the Supreme Court examined the law in *Bowsher v. Synar*. The Department of Justice's legal brief explicitly mentioned the "unitary Executive" and criticized independent agencies. During the oral arguments, statements in favor of the law seemed to suggest that the president could invalidate all independent agencies if he wanted to do so. Solicitor General Charles Fried then sought to dismiss that radical possibility as mere "scare tactics," to which Justice Sandra Day O'Connor replied, "Well, Mr. Fried, I'll confess you scared me with it."

Three months later, the Court ruled 7-2 that Gramm-Rudman was unconstitutional. Chief Justice Burger wrote,

> By placing the responsibility for execution of the Balanced Budget and Emergency Deficit Control Act in the hands of an officer who is subject to removal only by itself, Congress, in effect, has retained control over the execution of the Act, and has intruded into the executive function. The Constitution does not permit such intrusion.

Unitarians cheered the Court's decisions in *Chadha* and *Bowsher*, but the end of the Reagan presidency brought a case that unitarians would rue for decades, *Morrison v. Olson* (1988). The case touched on multiple constitutional questions but in particular the constitutionality of the independent counsel, per the special prosecutor provisions of the Ethics in Government Act (EIGA) of 1978, which had long irked unitarians because it gave the president only limited control over the independent counsel.

Indeed, in 1987 Reagan articulated criticisms of the EIGA because he could not remove the independent counsel. His signing statement to the 1987 reauthorization of the independent council complained about inadequate executive control: "An officer of the United States exercising executive authority in the core area of law enforcement necessarily, under our constitutional scheme, must be subject to executive branch appointment, review, and removal. There is no other constitutionally permissible alternative." Similarly, in October 1988 he pocket vetoed the Whistleblower Protection Act, which would have protected federal employees who report fraud and corruption, in part on the grounds that it would have rendered the Office of Special Counsel more independent of the executive.

Unitarians hoped that in *Morrison* the Court would finally get rid of the independent counsel as an unconstitutional intrusion on executive activities. In January 1988, the U.S. Court of Appeals for the District of Columbia ruled 2-1 that the independent counsel law was unconstitutional. The panel's ruling, which was written by Judge Lawrence Silberman, found that the law violated several aspects of the Constitution. It held that the Act violated the appointments clause of Article II, the limitations of Article III, and also the principle of separation of powers by interfering with the president's authority under Article II.

Silberman's opinion employed the term "unitary executive" 14 times in arguing for an executive unrestrained by Congress. It also invoked Alexander Hamilton in *Federalist* 70 and expressed frustration with *Humphrey's*. Silberman declared "Central to the government instituted by the Constitution are the doctrines of separation of powers and a unitary executive." He also noted a primary unitarian argument: "The Framers provided for a unitary executive to ensure that the branch wielding the power to enforce the law would be accountable to the people."

Several months after the DC Circuit's decision, the case reached the Supreme Court. During the 90 minutes of oral arguments at the Court, Solicitor General Charles Fried said, "Our central objection is that this statute strips the President of a purely executive function – criminal prosecution, and criminal prosecution in an important class of cases – and lodges that function in one almost wholly untethered to the President." But Fried also invoked the unitary executive, as he claimed that the special prosecutor statute threatened the existence of "a unitary, vigorous and independent Executive responsible directly to the people" that he said was essential to the functioning of the American system.

In June 1988, the Court rendered its decision in *Morrison*, ruling 7-1 that the 1978 Independent Counsel Act was constitutional. Chief Justice William Rehnquist wrote the majority opinion, which went against multiple unitary claims, reversing the main points that Silberman had made. Rehnquist said the law did not violate the president's constitutional appointment power, disputing the claim that "the 'good cause' removal provision at issue here impermissibly burdens the President's power to control or supervise the independent counsel, as an executive official, in the execution of his or her duties under the Act." Rehnquist also disagreed with the claim that "the Act, taken as a whole, violates the principle of separation of powers by unduly interfering with the role of the Executive Branch."

Justice Antonin Scalia was the lone dissenter in *Morrison*. His 38-page dissent set forth a principled argument for the unitary presidency. Scalia used the term "unitary executive" twice in his dissent. He wrote,

> the President's constitutionally assigned duties include *complete* control over investigation and prosecution of violations of the law, and that the inexorable command of Article II is clear and definite: the executive power must be vested in the President of the United States.

For Scalia, the vesting clause's grant "does not mean some of the executive power, but all of the executive power." He claimed that the majority had endorsed an ad hoc "fragmentation of executive power," and he lamented, "it is now open season upon the President's removal power for all executive officers." Scalia's dissent has resonated with unitarians ever since.

Scalia's dissent notwithstanding, *Morrison* was a sharp rebuke for unitarians. In essence, the Court in *Morrison* said that Congress could place officials in the executive branch who would be independent of the president. By extension, this meant that independent agencies were permissible; if an independent counsel is constitutional, so too must be an independent agency.

Thus, just as the doctrine of the unitary executive was officially born in the Reagan presidency, the Supreme Court seemed largely to strike it down late in Reagan's second term. Indeed, by some accounts (e.g., Savage, Divoll), *Morrison* effectively rejected the unitary executive. In 1989, Morton Rosenberg of the Congressional Research Service (CRS) wrote of the "demise of the Reagan Administration's theory of the unitary executive," as if it were over and done with at that point.

Nevertheless, the idea of the unitary executive did not die. As we will see, it rose again in the twenty-first century under George W. Bush, but it also reappeared in some fashion under the two presidents between Reagan and the second Bush.

After Reagan

George H.W. Bush

The unitary executive rose to prominence in the Reagan years, but it did not end with his presidency, as it was also a factor for the last two presidents of the twentieth century, George H.W. Bush and Bill Clinton. Even though some academic accounts treat the unitary executive in the late 1980s and 1990s as a relatively unimportant lull between the more dramatic controversies of the Reagan years and George W. Bush's presidency, there were a number of developments in this period that merit attention.

George H.W. Bush's presidency had more than a few unitarian actions. For example, Bush issued nearly as many signing statements during his four years in office as Reagan did during his eight years, and nearly 70% of them articulated principled constitutional objections to parts of the laws. Some of Bush's signing statements explicitly invoked his constitutional authority and responsibility "as head of a unitary executive branch" or "as head of the unitary executive branch."

In March 1989, Bush acted to further presidential control of the regulatory process, as his predecessors had done. He created the Council on Competitiveness, headed by Vice President Dan Quayle, to work with OIRA to review federal regulations and ensure that businesses were not unduly regulated. The council was controversial because it appeared to help businesses avoid regulation, its deliberations were not public, and it was not clear if the vice president could order an agency to change its regulations.

In July 1989, William Barr of Bush's OLC issued a dramatic memo on "common legislative encroachments on executive branch authority." The memo described and decried 10 "ways Congress most often intrudes or attempts to intrude into the functions and responsibilities assigned by the Constitution to the executive branch." It was largely a litany of unitarian complaints, such as congressional attempts to limit the president's removal power, to access sensitive executive information, to encroach on the president's power over foreign affairs, to delegate executive power to people outside the executive branch, to create commissions that are partly legislative and partly executive, and the legislative veto. The memo declared that "only by consistently and forcefully resisting such congressional incursions can executive branch prerogatives be preserved."

Additionally, Bush forced Congress to alter the April 1989 Whistle-blower Act by cutting the provisions about the Office of Special Counsel that had led to Reagan's pocket veto of the measure 6 months earlier. Bush also challenged congressional efforts to protect members of the Postal Service Board of Governors from being fired by the president. And he objected to part of the 1989 budget reconciliation act because it made requirements of the Secretary of Education that he claimed infringed upon the president's appointment authority.

Bill Clinton

The fact that George H.W. Bush's presidency exhibited some unitarian similarities with Reagan's is not altogether surprising, given their rough ideological similarity and Bush's eight years of service as Reagan's vice president before his own presidency. Yet, aspects of the unitary executive were also evident under Bill Clinton, who was the first Democratic president in twelve years. As several scholars (Rosen 2006; Krent 2008, 531; Barilleaux and Kelley 2010, 10) have claimed, Clinton did not trumpet the theory of the unitary executive, but he used it nevertheless.

For example, in May 1993 Clinton fired 7 people in the White House Travel Office. The employees technically serve at the pleasure of the president and therefore may be fired without cause, but Clinton's action violated the norm that such employees generally worked at the office for many years and remained in place even when a new president from a new party took office. The controversy led to investigations by the Department of Justice, GAO, Congress, and an independent counsel.

Clinton OLC officials Walter Dellinger and Randy Moss supported many of the claims of unitarians and vigorously fought against perceived encroachments upon executive power. In November 1993, the Clinton administration asked the Department of Justice for an opinion on presidential signing statements, which led to an opinion from Assistant Attorney General Dellinger that supported the president's ability to use signing statements to declare laws unconstitutional and called such a practice "a valid and reasonable exercise of Presidential authority." A year later, Dellinger wrote another memo on "Presidential Authority to Decline to Execute Unconstitutional Statutes."

And in 1996, Dellinger wrote a memo on "The Constitutional Separation of Powers Between the President and Congress." It was very much an echo of the Bush OLC memo of 1989, which it formally replaced, even though the Clinton memo stated, "we agree with many of the conclusions of that document." The new memo concluded that the executive branch must identify and resist legislative encroachments on its prerogatives:

> legislation that attempts to structure the very details of executive decision making, or that imposes onerous and repetitive reporting requirements on executive agencies, is troubling from a separation of powers standpoint even if the individual statutes could not easily be described in themselves as unconstitutional. The overall effects of such micromanagement for the constitutional separation of powers obviously can be tremendous, and yet it is unlikely that judicial intervention can or would preserve the constitutional balance. The executive branch thus has the primary responsibility for presenting, in as forceful and principled a way as possible, the separation of powers problems with all legislation that has such effects.

As Krent (2008, 532) notes, Clinton issued signing statements to push back against congressional encroachments on the president's nomination and appointment powers. For example, Clinton objected to the creation of an independent Social Security agency because its leader would be removable only for wrongdoing and not for political reasons. He objected to congressional directions to the Secretary of Transportation to create a Commercial Motor Vehicle Safety Regulatory Review Panel. And he objected to restrictions on his power to appoint the U.S. Trade Representative.

In November 2000, Clinton issued a signing statement in which he objected to limits on the president's power to remove the Director of the National Nuclear Safety Administration (NNSA). While most previous presidents' signing statements had articulated objections in general terms, Clinton's NNSA signing statement directly set out various executive actions that his administration would undertake in order to do what the president wanted even though that went against the legislative provisions.

Clinton also sought to enhance the president's role in regulatory review. His Executive Order 12,866 of October 1993 replaced Reagan's Executive Orders 12,291 and 12,498. It significantly expanded review of agency rulemaking by OMB to include independent regulatory agencies and commissions, just as Jimmy Carter had considered doing 15 years earlier. Clinton's regulatory efforts thus built upon but went beyond what his predecessors had done.

One year after serving as Clinton's Deputy Assistant for Domestic Policy but 9 years before she joined the Supreme Court, Elena Kagan reflected on the nature of Clinton's administrative efforts. In her view, Clinton created a new model of "presidential administration," which fell short of a truly unitarian executive but still entailed significant presidential influence. According to Kagan (2001, 2248):

> presidential control of administration, in critical respects, expanded dramatically during the Clinton years, making the regulatory activity of the executive branch agencies more and more an extension of the President's own policy and political agenda. Faced for most of his time in office with a hostile Congress but eager to show progress on domestic issues, Clinton and his White House staff turned to the bureaucracy to achieve, to the extent it could, the full panoply of his domestic policy goals.

Although Clinton's presidency thus exhibited some unitarian tendencies, in other respects it shied away from the unitary executive. For example, although Clinton initially refused to disclose who had met with First Lady Hillary Clinton's task force on health care reform, he later relented and released the names of over 500 people who were involved, in part because many of them had already been identified. And Clinton did not turn to the unitary executive or forcefully invoke executive privilege or challenge the constitutionality of a presidential subpoena to avoid testifying before a grand jury in August 1998 about his relationships with Paula Jones and Monica Lewinsky – testimony that led to his impeachment later that year.

Conclusion

This chapter has covered the highlights of the development of the unitary executive over the last two decades of the twentieth century, from its birth as an explicit and controversial doctrine under Ronald Reagan to its less pronounced, but still significant, status under George H.W. Bush and Bill Clinton. By the close of the twentieth century, unitarians could point not only to various de facto precedents before Reagan, but also to various explicitly unitarian actions under Reagan, as well as to some generally unitarian actions under Reagan's two successors. This era thus saw the unitary executive transition from a mere theoretical possibility with vague historical antecedents, to a contested political reality, to what was arguably a constitutional setback, followed by an uneasy but quieter continuation into the twenty-first century.

3
THE UNITARY EXECUTIVE IN THE TWENTY-FIRST CENTURY

This chapter explores the unitary executive in the twenty-first century, from George W. Bush's avowedly and vigorously unitary presidency, to its less prominent status under Barack Obama, to its quasi-revival under Donald Trump. As we will see, the unitary executive in this period exhibits both continuities with and changes from its late twentieth century version.

George W. Bush

If Ronald Reagan's presidency marked the birth of the unitary executive as an explicit doctrine, then George W. Bush's presidency marked some of its boldest claims to date. Indeed, after the relative calm of the George H.W. Bush and Bill Clinton presidencies, the unitary executive returned to prominence and great controversy under George W. Bush, who used it far more frequently and forcefully than even Reagan had.

Why Did Bush Embrace the Unitary Executive?

Before examining George W. Bush's many unitary actions, it might be useful to consider the reason(s) behind those actions. While no one denies that Bush embraced the unitary executive theory, there is some disagreement about why he did so. There are several plausible reasons for the Bush administration's invocation of the unitary executive theory.

On one view (Skowronek 2009, 2099), Bush turned to the unitary executive theory because of the contested presidential election of 2000.

Whereas most presidents enter office with a political mandate for action based on having received a majority of the votes, Bush's opponent Al Gore received 543,895 more votes, and Bush's narrow electoral victory was not clear until the Supreme Court's controversial ruling in *Bush v. Gore* decided the winner in Florida 5 weeks after Election Day. Under those circumstances, Bush lacked a political mandate for what he wanted to do. Yet, the unitary executive theory permitted him to claim that the presidential office itself permitted him to do what he wanted.

On another view (Genovese 2011, 133), Bush turned to the unitary executive theory because it enabled him to respond forcefully to the terrorist attacks of September 11, 2001. The deaths of nearly 3,000 people on American soil traumatized the nation and called out for some sort of strong response. Insofar as that response was one that the normal governance system was ill-prepared to make, the unitary executive theory offered a justification for the sort of extraordinary actions that Bush felt were necessary under the circumstances. By some accounts (e.g., Mayer 2006), Bush's invocation of the unitary executive was part of the "New Paradigm," an approach designed to help the president respond to the 9/11 attacks by quickly bringing terrorists to justice. The phrase comes from a memo by White House Counsel Alberto Gonzalez of January 25, 2002 about the new exigencies of the war on terrorism. Gonzalez's memo sought to stake out a wide range for presidential action free from traditional restraints, saying "this new paradigm renders obsolete Geneva's strict limitations on questioning of enemy prisoners and renders quaint some of its provisions …"

A third view (Fisher 2010, 588, 591; Genovese 2011; Crouch et al. 2013, 561) is that Bush used the unitary executive theory just for convenient rhetorical cover to permit him to do what he wanted. In other words, it was neither the unusual nature of Bush's election nor the devastation of 9/11 that drove him to the unitary executive theory, it was simple run-of-the-mill political convenience. Like other presidents, Bush wanted to do things, and the ordinary means towards his ends were cumbersome (e.g., legislation), so the unitary executive offered an easy post hoc justification for opportune presidential action. According to Genovese, "the Bush presidency was compelled to move beyond its bold power assertions and present a political and intellectual justification of its unilateral actions. The result was the development of the 'unitary executive.'" Thus, Bush used the unitary executive theory as a "legal fig leaf, behind which all manner of presidential action could be justified" (Genovese 2011, 130).

Last but not least, some scholars (MacKenzie 2008, 33; Barilleaux and Kelley 2010, 222; Crouch et al. 2013, 564; Rozell and Sollenberger 2013, 37) see Bush's invocation of the unitary executive theory as rooted in a sincere desire to reinvigorate the presidency, to restore power that had been wrongly wrested from it in the 1970s. Vice President Dick Cheney was central to promoting this idea. As Cheney saw it, presidential power had been hurt by Congress's overreactions to Nixon. Cheney had worked in the Nixon and Ford White Houses, so he had seen up close how an assertive Congress tried to curtail the executive. As Cheney said in an interview in 2005:

> I do have the view that over the years there had been an erosion of presidential power and authority ... A lot of the things around Watergate and Vietnam both, in the 1970s, served to erode the authority I think the president needs to be effective, especially in the national security area.

Cheney's conception of a radically reduced presidency post-Nixon was debatable, as some would regard Congress's push-back against Nixon's various misdeeds as entirely appropriate, while others would point to various assertive presidential actions in the 1980s, yet that was Cheney's sincere view.

There is some evidence for each of the above reasons for Bush's embrace of the unitary executive, and their relative persuasiveness may well depend on how generously one is inclined to view Bush's presidency. Regardless of why the Bush administration promoted the unitary executive theory, it was embraced by Cheney, John Yoo, David Addington, Jay Bybee, and Alberto Gonzales, among others in the Bush administration, and it was a significant part of Bush's eight years in office.

Bush's Unitary Actions

At times, Bush's own rhetoric very much aligned with the unitary executive theory. For example, as Bush said in 2006 about not firing Secretary of Defense Donald Rumsfeld, "I'm the decider." Bush also told journalist Bob Woodward that he did not need to explain his decisions: "I do not need to explain why I say things. That's the interesting thing about being the president. Maybe somebody needs to explain to me why they say something, but I don't feel I owe anybody an explanation." And in 2017 Bush told author Mark Updegrove that contrary to the perception that Dick Cheney and Donald Rumsfeld had effectively made a lot of important decisions in his administration, they "didn't make one f---ing decision" and that he alone had called all the shots.

The Bush administration explicitly referenced the unitary executive theory dozens of times and relied on it to expand its powers in terms of executive branch czars, executive privilege, the removal power, regulation, signing statements, and foreign affairs, among other things.

Czars

Bush made extensive use of unofficial "czars," or aides who advise the president and help coordinate policy efforts without having to utilize the traditional system of congressionally approved officials. For some, the use of czars was just another aspect of what was by then a "four-decade trend of extending White House control over the executive branch" (Barilleaux and Kelley 2010, 219–220). But for others, the practice raised constitutional concerns, as czars enhance the president's ability to make public policy at the expense of Congress. For example, Sollenberger and Rozell (2012, 3) say that czars can be "a direct violation of the core principles of a system of separation of powers and government accountability." Regardless, Bush used three dozen executive branch czars for issues like faith-based initiatives, homeland security, technology, Gulf Coast reconstruction, and health care.

Secrecy

In several instances, Bush refused to give Congress information, per the doctrine of executive privilege. In 2002, the Bush administration refused to release information regarding Bill Clinton's late-term pardons, even though Clinton himself did not oppose the release. Also, in 2002, in an artful combination of the unitary use of czars and secrecy, Bush refused to let Homeland Security Advisor Tom Ridge testify before Congress, on the debatable grounds that at the time Ridge was a presidential advisor, not (yet) a cabinet officer. The Bush administration also resisted providing information regarding the public identification of Valerie Plame as a covert CIA operative in 2003 and the firing of U.S. attorneys in 2006.

In 2004, during arguments before the Supreme Court about whether the administration could be forced to divulge information regarding Cheney's 2001 energy task force (*Cheney v. U.S. District Court*), Solicitor General Ted Olson argued that the other two branches could not force the presidents to disclose information, including the limited sort of information routinely used in the legal discovery process. Olson said, "We're submitting that discovery itself violates the Constitution."

Near the end of his presidency, Bush invoked executive privilege to keep Congress from obtaining documents about the EPA's decision not to let California regulate greenhouse gas emissions from automobiles. Attorney General Michael Mukasey argued that since the decision involved discussions with the White House, he could withhold the documents.

Altogether, the Bush administration's invocations of executive privilege and its other efforts to control information were more assertive than had been the norm previously. According to Rozell and Sollenberger (2013, 45),

> The administration, under the guidance of the unitary executive theory, sought to vastly expand and combine the traditional categories of executive privilege in ways that, if successful, would have ultimately walled off the executive branch from any system of accountability.

Removal Power

Early in the Bush administration, the White House asked OLC for an opinion about whether the president could fire the incumbent Chair of the Consumer Product Safety Commission (CPSC). John Yoo said yes, invoking an old legal view that "The power to remove is the power to control." Yoo's memo of July 2001 argued that the president enjoyed a broad power of removal, yet it also pointed to statutory language that appeared not to explicitly preclude removal by the president. His memo said, "We conclude that the Chairman of the CPSC serves at the pleasure of the President, and that the President has the constitutional authority to remove her for any reason."

In 2002, Bush insisted on the ability to remove all 170,000 workers at the new Department of Homeland Security, contrary to the usual collective bargaining rights and civil service protections for federal employees. And in 2006, Attorney General Alberto Gonzales fired seven U.S. Attorneys. The move was a dramatic break with tradition that seemed driven by a presidential desire for greater political control over the Department of Justice, and critics charged that the firings threatened prosecutorial independence. In the ensuing uproar, it became clear that the firings were politically motivated, and numerous officials had to step down, ultimately including Karl Rove and Alberto Gonzales.

Regulatory Review

Like its immediate predecessors, the Bush administration sought to strengthen the president's role in the regulatory process. In 2001, OIRA administrator John Graham issued a memo to create a "prompt letter" program, via which OIRA could proactively suggest that agencies make certain regulations, rather than just react after regulations had been initiated. Over the next three years OIRA issued 15 prompt letters, many of which led to agency action.

In 2007, Bush issued Executive Order 13,422 to enact several important changes to the process of regulatory review. The order sought to further presidential control of the regulatory process. It required agencies to identify a "specific market failure" that warranted the regulation and to calculate the costs and benefits of each individual regulation and of all regulations in a given year. It also called for each agency to have a Regulatory Policy Officer (RPO), who would facilitate the administration's agenda. And it extended presidential review by covering the many guidance documents that agencies issue to articulate how they will interpret or enforce rules and regulations. In June 2007, the House of Representatives responded to Executive Order 13,422 by voting to prohibit OIRA from using funds to implement it.

Signing Statements

Although Bill Clinton issued more signing statements than Bush did, Bush issued more that asserted presidential authority to bypass statutory provisions. Bush used signing statements dozens of times, challenging over a thousand provisions of laws. And in many instances his signing statements explicitly invoked the unitary executive as the reason for opposing legislative provisions.

For example, in his signing statement for a defense authorization bill in December 2001, Bush wrote, "These provisions shall be implemented in a manner consistent with the President's constitutional authority to supervise the unitary executive branch and to recommend to the Congress such measures as the President judges necessary and expedient." Dozens of Bush's signing statements contained similar language. Bush's signing statement for the 2006 defense authorization act mentioned the unitary executive twice.

One of Bush's best-known signing statements undercut the so-called McCain amendment about the (im)permissibility of torture in the 2005 Detainee Treatment Act. Bush's statement said, "The executive branch shall construe Title X in Division A of the Act, relating to detainees, in a manner consistent with the constitutional authority of the President to supervise the unitary executive branch and as Commander in Chief ..." As an anonymous senior Bush official explained Bush's statement,

Of course the president has the obligation to follow this law, [but] he also has the obligation to defend and protect the country as the commander in chief, and he will have to square those two responsibilities ... We are not expecting that those two responsibilities will come into conflict, but it's possible that they will.

According to Richard Conley (2011, 47), "For Bush, signing statements constituted a key component of the administration's articulation of the principle of the 'unitary executive' or the concept of unfettered presidential authority over the executive branch." And Rick Waterman (2009, 6–7) notes, "In his extravagant use of signing statements ... Bush unilaterally created what essentially amounted to a line-item veto." By one indication, Bush's efforts were successful: a 2007 GAO report that found federal agencies ignored 30% of the laws to which Bush's signing statements had objected.

Alito

Debates about the unitary executive also came up when Bush nominated Samuel Alito to the Supreme Court in 2005. Alito had served in the Reagan administration and been among the many people there who had advocated the unitary executive theory and had continued to do so subsequently. Indeed, in 2000, Alito told the Federalist Society:

We were strong proponents of the theory of the unitary executive, that all federal executive power is vested by the Constitution in the president. And I thought then, and I still think, that this theory best captures the meaning of the Constitution's text and structure.

Alito also said that the unitary executive was the "gospel according to OLC."

Alito's support of the unitary executive was a major issue during his Senate confirmation hearings in January 2006. Senator Arlen Specter (then-R, PA) asked Alito about a memo he had authored while working for Reagan's OLC in 1986 on the benefits for the executive branch of an increased use of presidential signing statements. Alito's 20-year old memo said, "Since the president's approval is just as important as that of the House or Senate, it seems to follow that the president's understanding of the bill should be just as important as that of Congress." In his response to Specter, Alito claimed that the issue had been merely "theoretical." Despite this assurance, Senator Dianne Feinstein (D, CA) ultimately opposed Alito's nomination in part because of his adherence to the unitary executive theory, instead of what she regarded as "a proper system of checks and balances."

Changes in the Unitary Executive Under Bush

As the previous discussion demonstrates, Bush embraced the theory of the unitary executive and used it to justify a variety of controversial actions. Some of those actions echoed and built upon earlier precedents and practices, but others went beyond them. Indeed, many commentators claim that under Bush the unitary executive theory was quite different from its earlier manifestations. Academic treatments of Bush's version of the unitary executive theory have variously described it as new, novel, unorthodox, bold, radical, extreme, a sea change, a quantum expansion, super-sized, super-strong, strained, and monarchical. Some of those characterizations may be hyperbolic, but there was something different in the unitary executive under Bush.

Bush's Unitary Executive and Foreign Policy

One difference in Bush's use of the unitary executive was a substantive extension into new territory, moving from the domestic and administrative areas in which it had traditionally been used to new justifications for various foreign policy and national security matters. The radical nature of the Bush administration's claims of executive power in the foreign policy realm can be seen in official memos authored by its legal team, particularly the so-called "torture memos" and related documents. As previously discussed, Gonzalez's memo of January 25, 2002 described the "new paradigm" of the war on terror, which supposedly rendered the Geneva Conventions "quaint" and "obsolete."

On August 1, 2002, Assistant Attorney General Jay Bybee issued a memo on the permissibility of torture that staked out a wide if not unlimited presidential power over foreign policy. The memo described "the President's complete authority over the conduct of war" (34) and claimed "the president enjoys complete discretion in the exercise of his Commander-in-Chief authority" (33). Bybee mentioned Hamilton's view in *Federalist* 23 about the expansive nature of the President's authority to ensure the country's security and said "there can be no limitation of that authority, which is to provide for the defense and protection of the community, in any matter essential to its efficacy" (37). Bybee argued, "Just as statutes that order the President to conduct warfare in a certain manner or for specific goals would be unconstitutional, so too are laws that seek to prevent the President from gaining the intelligence he believes necessary to prevent attacks upon the United States" (39).

John Yoo's memo of September 25, 2001 made other bold claims about presidential power. Written just two weeks after 9/11, Yoo's memo repeatedly claimed that the president had "plenary" power over foreign affairs. It declared that president had "plenary constitutional power to take such military actions as he deems necessary and appropriate to respond to the terrorist attacks." Yoo's memo also stated, "In the exercise of his plenary power to use military force, the President's decisions are for him alone and are nonreviewable."

Nevertheless, the memo argued that the other branches of government had assented to the president's supremacy. As for the legislative branch, Yoo noted Congress's post-9/11 authorization and said, "Congress's support for the President's power suggests no limits on the Executive's judgment whether to use military force in response to the national emergency." As for the judiciary, Yoo invoked several cases to assert that courts had accepted that the president's power in foreign affairs was complete and exclusive. Based on these arguments, Yoo declared, "Our review shows that all three branches of the Federal Government – Congress, the Executive, and the Judiciary – agree that the President has broad authority to use military force abroad, including the ability to deter future attacks."

In making those and other points, Yoo's memo explicitly mentioned the unitary executive multiple times. For instance, it said:

> It is clear that the Constitution secures all federal executive power in the President to ensure a unity in purpose and energy in action. 'Decision, activity, secrecy, and dispatch will generally characterize the proceedings of one man in a much more eminent degree than the proceedings of any greater number.' The Federalist No. 70, at 392 (Alexander Hamilton). The centralization of authority in the President alone is particularly crucial in matters of national defense, war, and foreign policy, where a unitary executive can evaluate threats, consider policy choices, and mobilize national resources with a speed and energy that is far superior to any other branch. As Hamilton noted, 'Energy in the executive is a leading character in the definition of good government. It is essential to the protection of the community against foreign attacks.' Id. at 391. This is no less true in war. 'Of all the cares or concerns of government, the direction of war most peculiarly demands those qualities which distinguish the exercise of power by a single hand.' Id. No. 74, at 415 (Alexander Hamilton).

Inherent Power

The Bush administration's extension of the unitary executive theory to the realm of foreign policy was one respect in which its use of the theory was different, but it was not the only way in which it differed. Some commentators (e.g., Savage 2007; Calabresi and Yoo 2008, 428; Crouch et al. 2017, 564) also perceived a thematic expansion of the theory to include inherent powers.

Once again, the memos of Bush's legal team are instructive. John Yoo's memo of September 25, 2001 repeatedly claimed that the president possessed inherent powers. Yoo said, "the President's powers include inherent executive powers that are unenumerated in the Constitution." He also said, "We conclude that the President has broad constitutional power to use military force. Congress has acknowledged this inherent executive power."

The idea of inherent presidential power also appeared in *Hamdan v. Rumsfeld* (2006). As the Department of Justice put it in a legal brief for the case, "the President has the inherent authority to convene military commissions to try and punish captured enemy combatants in wartime – even in the absence of any statutory authorization." Marouf Hasian (2007, 702) maintains that in *Hamdan* the Bush administration officials were "often treating 'inherent' commander-in-chief powers as though they originate from some metaphysical, natural sources that may not be represented in written constitutions or statutes." In his majority opinion in the case, Justice John Paul Stevens wrote in a footnote, "Whether or not the President has independent power, absent congressional authorization, to convene military commissions, he may not disregard limitations that Congress has, in proper exercise of its own war powers, placed on his powers."

Journalist Charlie Savage (2007, 124, 273) invoked the popular old advertisement for Reese's Peanut Butter Cups to describe how the unitary executive may be combined with the idea of inherent executive power to produce something greater than the sum of the two parts. Just as chocolate and peanut butter can be delicious on their own terms but when combined they are perhaps even better, the two accounts of executive power similarly produce a potent combination. According to Savage (2007), the idea of inherent power increases the range of what the president can do, and the unitary executive theory holds that Congress cannot place restrictions on how the president executes executive functions: "When fused, the two theories transformed any conceivably executive power into an exclusive one. The president could do virtually anything, without any check by Congress."

Criticism

As might be expected, the Bush administration's assertive invocations of the unitary executive theory for both domestic and foreign policy, as well as its claims to inherent powers, met with considerable criticism. For example, in April 2006, Savage published an exposé on Bush's use of signing statements, claiming that Bush had used the devices to ignore over 750 legislative requirements. Members of the Senate Judiciary Committee then complained about the practice and in June 2006 held hearings on signing statements.

In August 2006, the American Bar Association (ABA) stepped into the debate about signing statements. The ABA's Task Force on Presidential Signing Statements and the Separation of Powers Doctrine issued a report, noting that Bush's use of signing statements was tied to his views about the unitary executive. The task force concluded that Bush's signing statements could well "weaken our cherished system of checks and balances and separation of powers."

In early 2007, the House Committee on the Judiciary initiated an investigation of Bush's signing statements and explicitly discussed how the practice was driven by the unitary executive theory. In the 110th Congress (2007–2009), a Democratic House Member introduced legislation to curtail the use of presidential signing statements, and a Republican Senator introduced a bill that would have rejected specific parts of one of Bush's signing statements.

Bush's use of the unitary executive theory was also criticized by people who were previously proponents of the theory. For example, Steven Calabresi and Christopher Yoo expressed concern with how Bush had used the theory. They were particularly troubled by how the Bush administration tied the unitary executive theory to the idea of inherent power. They conceded that "on occasion presidents have asserted claims of inherent executive powers that far surpassed the powers of direction, nullification, and removal implicit in the classic theory of the unitary executive" (18), but in their view "the conclusion with respect to these broader claims of inherent executive power in times of emergency is very different from the one we draw with respect to claims of inherent presidential power to control the execution of laws by subordinates" (19). According to Calabresi and Yoo (19–20),

> the Bush administration's claims of broad, inherent executive power stand on footing in terms of the Constitution's text and ratification history that is very different from the basis of the theory of the unitary executive that grew out of the frustrations of the ineffective plural executives of the early state constitutions as well as the 'executive committee' established by the Articles of Confederation.

Therefore, they charge that "Bush has discredited the theory of the unitary executive by associating it not with presidential authority to remove and direct subordinate executive officials but with implied, inherent foreign policy powers, some of which, at least, the president simply does not possess ..." (429).

Bush's robust unitarianism was criticized not just by politicians and traditional unitarians, but also by the judiciary. In *Hamdan v. Rumsfeld* (2006), the Court rejected the military commissions created by the Bush administration to try suspected terrorists at Guantanamo, and by some accounts thereby also rejected extreme presidentialism, or at least the idea of extensive inherent presidential power. Former Clinton-era Solicitor General Walter Dellinger called *Hamdan* "the most important decision on presidential power and the rule of law ever."

Furthermore, many observers (e.g., Mackenzie 2008, 55) claim that the *Hamdan* decision rejected Bush's unitary arguments. As Hasian (2007, 705) notes, "Countless academicians, journalists, and politicians viewed the *Hamdan* decision as a direct repudiation of what some called the 'strained,' 'novel,' or unorthodox 'theory' of the unitary executive." In particular, Hasian sees the dissent of Clarence Thomas in *Hamdan* as very unitarian. Thomas took the unusual step of reading his dissenting opinion from the bench. It referenced the advantages of "unity" in the executive and also referenced his dissent in *Hamdi v. Rumsfeld* (2004), which itself explicitly referenced the unitary executive.

As the above points indicate, altogether Bush's use of the unitary executive theory made what was already a controversial theory even more controversial.

Barack Obama

By the end of George W. Bush's presidency, the unitary executive theory was arguably sullied by its connection to a highly unpopular president, its own image tarnished by its association with his. There was reason to think that the unitary executive theory might end with Bush's presidency, that its revival in the early twenty-first century would be relegated to the history books as an artifact of an unusual president and unusual times. But just as the unitary executive did not die after the Court's decision in *Morrison v. Olson* in 1988, it did not disappear after George W. Bush.

The question of presidential power was a factor in the 2008 presidential election, as many Americans felt the Bush administration had been heavy-handed and overly unilateral. During the buildup to the presidential primaries in late 2007, Hillary Clinton told the *Boston Globe* that she did not subscribe to the "unitary executive" theory, which she saw as having been pushed by Dick Cheney. She claimed, "It has been a concerted effort by the vice president, with the full acquiescence of the president, to create a much more powerful executive at the expense of both branches of government and of the American people." Clinton also said, "I think you have to restore the checks and balances and the separation of powers, which means reining in the presidency."

As a presidential candidate, Barack Obama also criticized Bush's alleged excesses in presidential power. And in the vice presidential debate in October 2008, Joe Biden claimed that due to Cheney's embrace of the unitary executive theory, "Vice President Cheney has been the most dangerous vice president we've had probably in American history." Similarly, in December 2008, then Vice President-Elect Biden told a journalist that he disagreed with Cheney's support for the unitary executive: "His notion of a unitary executive, meaning that in time of war, essentially all power goes to the executive, I think is dead wrong, I think is mistaken."

Beyond generic comments against the unitary executive theory, candidate Obama also criticized some of the particular actions that Bush undertook in its name. For example, in late 2007, Obama told the *Boston Globe* that "it is a clear abuse of power" for the president to issue a signing statement "to evade laws that the president does not like or as an end-run around provisions designed to foster accountability."

Early in his presidency, Obama echoed some of the criticisms he had made during the campaign about Bush's unilateralism. For example, in March 2009, Obama issued a memorandum on the use of presidential signing statements. Directed to the heads of executive agencies and departments, it said that Obama would use signing statements only to raise serious constitutional concerns and not to direct officials to disregard provisions he disliked. And in his second term, Obama repeatedly asked Congress to authorize U.S. military action in Syria against ISIS, even though Congress refused to do so. Thus, unlike Bush, Obama made no claim of unitary or inherent presidential military power and instead sought traditional legislative approval.

Yet, even though Obama generally shied away from confrontational unilateralism and did not trumpet the unitary executive theory like his predecessor, some scholars (e.g., Barilleaux and Maxwell 2017, 32; Crouch et al. 2017, 562, 568) contend that he nevertheless undertook several actions that were consistent with adherence to the theory of the unitary executive. For example, like Bush, Obama appointed "czars" to centralize power in the White House and to coordinate policy efforts in various areas. In 200 Members of Congress wrote letters to the president to complain about his extensive use of czars. In February 2009, Senator Robert Byrd (D, WV) wrote to the president:

> The rapid and easy accumulation of power by White House staff can threaten the Constitutional system of checks and balances. At the worst, White House staff have taken direction and control of programmatic areas that are the statutory responsibility of Senate-confirmed officials.

In May 2009, Senator John McCain (R, AZ) quipped that "Obama has more czars than the Romanovs – who ruled Russia for 3 centuries." In September 2009, six Republicans identified 18 czars and complained that they "may be undermining the constitutional oversight responsibilities of Congress."

Obama also undertook other actions which were essentially unitary. For example, he issued several notable signing statements. On multiple occasions, he issued signing statements for defense authorization acts so that he could ignore statutory requirements to notify Congress before moving detainees from Guantanamo. Obama was also aggressive with recess appointments during pro forma Senate sessions, leading to a unanimous rebuke from the Court in *NLRB v. Noel Canning* (2014). When Congress failed to enact immigration reform, in 2012 Obama granted an administrative amnesty from deportation for hundreds of thousands of "Dreamers," or undocumented immigrants who came to the United States as children. Obama also repeatedly delayed the enforcement of parts of the Affordable Care Act (Obamacare). On multiple occasions, he extended or waived requirements regarding the employer mandate, enrollment deadlines, and high-risk pools, and he also did not enforce requirements for small businesses and state health exchanges. In terms of controlling information, in January 2012 Obama invoked executive privilege to withhold information on the ATF's "fast and furious" gun program from Congress, and he repeatedly invoked the state secrets privilege.

In terms of regulatory review, Obama continued the practice of seeking greater presidential control over regulation and rulemaking. His Executive Order 13,653 of January 2011 added qualitative considerations to cost-benefit analyses and required agencies to retrospectively review their existing regulations, and he issued several executive orders that required departments and agencies to address environmental sustainability and climate change. In 2011, Obama rejected an EPA proposal to tighten the standards for ozone pollution, allegedly to avoid angering businesses in advance of his reelection bid. And in 2015 he publicly pressured the independent FCC to declare the Internet a public utility that could be regulated.

In short, while the Obama presidency provided a respite from the explicit and vigorous assertions of the unitary executive of the Bush years, it also suggested that the doctrine was not altogether dormant, let alone dead.

Donald Trump

After the relative quiet of Obama's presidency, the unitary executive view reappeared in the Trump administration. It can be difficult to discern a clear stance toward the unitary executive in the Trump presidency, but Trump and his administration have demonstrated an affinity for the unitary executive. The concept of the unitary executive arguably comports with Trump's personality, his admiration of autocratic leaders, his penchant for bold personal decision-making, and his desire for loyalty. Of course, the unitary executive under Trump might also be related to his lack of a political mandate following his surprise electoral victory in 2016, or to the imperatives of the contemporary presidential office.

Trump's Words

Trump and his aides have made a number of rhetorical invocations of the unitary executive, both implicitly and explicitly. Trump often talks in way that accords with the idea of the unitary executive. For example, in his presidential-announcement speech in 2015, Trump made a great many references to himself, using the first-person pronoun "I" hundreds of times. This speech gave an early indication of candidate's pronounced individualism and his focus on himself. Trump's proclamation at the 2016 Republican National Convention that "I alone can fix it" evoked the same personal embodiment of executive power that unitarians hold. Similarly, in November 2017, Trump declared, "The one that matters is me. I'm the only one who matters."

During the GOP primaries, Trump was asked if the military would follow a controversial order to target terrorists' families. Trump said, "If I say do it, they're gonna do it. That's what leadership is all about." And shortly after meeting with North Korea's leader Kim Jong Un in June 2018, Trump told a reporter: "He's the head of the country. And I mean he's the strong head. Don't let anyone think anything different. He speaks and his people sit up at attention. I want my people to do the same."

While pronouncements like those above suggest that Trump has a basic affinity with the theory of the unitary executive, Trump's lawyers have explicitly invoked the doctrine. For example, when asked in June 2017 if Trump would fire special counsel Robert Mueller in order to stop his investigation of Russian interference in the 2016 election, Jay Sekulow, a member of Trump's legal team, said, "Look, the president of the United States, as we all know, is a unitary executive," suggesting that Trump had the right to fire anyone for any reason.

A memo from Trump legal team member Marc Kasowitz to Robert Mueller of June 23, 2017 also explicitly invoked the unitary executive: "As a Constitutional matter, the President also possesses the indisputable authority to direct that any executive branch investigation be open or closed because the Constitution provides for a unitary executive with all executive power resting with the President."

Trump's Deeds

Beyond Trump's words, the unitary executive also accords with some of his deeds, relating to long-held unitary concerns like secrecy, the control and removal of subordinates, signing statements, and claims about the nature and scope of presidential power.

Controlling Information

Trump has acted in several ways to further presidential control of information and secrecy. For example, he required dozens of White House aides to sign nondisclosure agreements, presumably to limit his subordinates' ability to talk about their work for the president. A more dramatic example of the Trump administration's efforts to control information occurred in January 2018 when former White House strategist Steve Bannon testified before the House Intelligence Committee. At several points during Bannon's testimony, his attorney took breaks to confer via telephone with the White House counsel's office to clarify what questions could be answered. Each time he came back with the same guidance: Bannon could not discuss any activities related to the transition or his tenure in the White House.

Also in January 2018, Trump's legal team wrote a confidential letter to special counsel Robert Mueller arguing that executive privilege would enable the president to avoid having to provide testimony, so as to block a possible future subpoena of the president. In April 2018, Trump's lawyers demanded to review the evidence that the FBI seized from Trump's personal lawyer Michael Cohen. They said the president, rather than legal investigators, could best determine which documents should be covered by attorney-client privilege. And in May 2018, Trump pressured intelligence and law enforcement officials to allow congressional Republicans to view highly classified information related to the Russia investigation that the officials had refused to divulge.

The Removal Power

The former host of *The Apprentice*, Trump has not hesitated to say, "You're fired." Thus far, the list of high-ranking officials whom Trump had fired includes Jim Mattis, Jeff Sessions, David Shulkin, H.R. McMaster, John McEntee, Rex Tillerson, Andrew McCabe, Steve Bannon, Anthony Scaramucci, Reince Priebus, James Comey, Michael Flynn, and Sally Yates, among others. There are also many people whom the president has threatened to fire, and many who have effectively been forced to resign.

Signing Statements

Thus far, Trump has issued a couple dozen presidential signing statements. Many of them are more in the mode of crass political pronouncements than principled statements about the laws, but some have followed the unitary practice of asserting the president's own constitutional judgments. For example, in May 2017 in his first signing statement, Trump said that he was reserving the right to disregard 89 parts of the law he had just signed. According to signing statement scholar Christopher Kelley (quoted in Korte), "This is a George W. Bush-style signing statement ... It's a line-by-line series of objections that lead to dozens and dozens of challenges that you just did not see in the Obama administration."

In August 2017, when Congress passed a Russia sanctions bill, Trump issued two signing statements, both of which challenged Congress on constitutional grounds. The first statement said, "In its haste to pass this legislation the Congress included a number of clearly unconstitutional provisions." The second statement called the bill "seriously flawed" because "it encroaches on the executive branch's authority."

And in December 2017, after signing into law a defense bill, Trump claimed "the bill includes several provisions that raise constitutional concerns." For example, Trump wrote, "Several provisions of the bill ... purport to restrict the President's authority to control the personnel and materiel the President believes is necessary or advisable for the successful conduct of military missions." He also wrote that some provisions were inconsistent with executive privilege, therefore "My Administration will treat these provisions consistent with the President's constitutional authority to withhold information."

Bold Claims of Power

Trump has made several bold claims about presidential powers that accord with the theory of the unitary executive. Trump's early controversial executive orders banning immigration from majority Muslim countries produced some such claims. According to Crouch et al. (2017, 570),

> The travel ban executive order is a classic example of the unitary executive mindset. Not only did the Trump administration claim superiority in the realm of national security, but it also argued that the court did not have the ability to even review the constitutionality of the president's action.

Another unitarian action by Trump concerned the Consumer Financial Protection Bureau (CFPB). In 2017, the CFPB's director resigned and named his own replacement, while Trump named another person to be the acting director until confirmed by the Senate. Neither official recognized the other, leaving the agency with two putative leaders. The problem was rooted in the broader struggle between the president and Congress over who controls the federal bureaucracy, and the CFPB was created to be fairly autonomous. In late 2017, a federal judge upheld Trump's right to name the director, a decision that critics feared would erode the independence of the bureau and bring it more under presidential control. However, in early 2018, a federal appeals court ruled that the president could fire the director only "for cause," rather than for political reasons. The court said, "Congress's decision to provide the C.F.P.B. director a degree of insulation reflects its permissible judgment that civil regulation of consumer financial protection should be kept one step removed from political winds and presidential will."

In late 2017 and early 2018, Trump's legal team made the remarkable claim that the president cannot obstruct justice. In December 2017, Trump's personal attorney John Dowd claimed that the "President cannot obstruct justice because he is the chief law enforcement officer under

[Article II] and has every right to express his view of any case." In a follow-up interview, Dowd said that the president "has more power and discretion on that matter tha[n] DOJ and FBI put together. He cannot obstruct himself!" Similarly, in January 2018, Trump's legal team pushed back against the notion that Trump might have obstructed justice by seeking to thwart the investigation of Russian meddling in the 2016 election. Dowd wrote a memo that said,

> No FBI investigation was or even could have been obstructed. It remains our position that the President's actions here, by virtue of his position as the chief law enforcement officer, could neither constitutionally nor legally constitute obstruction because that would amount to him obstructing himself.

For many observers, the claim that the president could not logically obstruct justice was very much akin to Richard Nixon's infamous boast that "when the president does it, that means that it is not illegal."

Trump has also invoked a rather robust understanding of the president's pardon power. In July 2017, Trump declared that he possessed "complete" pardon power, and in January 2018 he claimed "I have the absolute right to pardon myself." Critics have charged that the president cannot pardon himself, nor could he promise to pardon underlings on the condition that they do as the president wishes. Similarly, in January 2019, Trump claimed that he possessed "the absolute right to declare a national emergency" in order to build a wall along the border with Mexico.

In terms of foreign affairs and the use of the military, Trump's claims of power echo those of the George W. Bush administration. For example, in October 2017, Defense Secretary James Mattis told the Senate Foreign Relations Committee that the president did not require authorization from Congress in order to target al-Qaeda, the Taliban, or ISIS, saying "It lies firmly within any president's constitutional authority and responsibility as the elected commander-in-chief." In a memo signed March 31, 2018, Assistant Attorney General Steven Engel defended the president's decision to fire cruise missiles at a Syrian airfield in April 2017, saying "The President had the constitutional authority to carry out the proposed airstrikes" because "they did not amount to war in the constitutional sense and therefore did not require prior congressional approval." Such claims are close to the Bush-era claims of inherent presidential power to direct military action.

The Trump administration has also pursued the unitary idea of control over executive officials in terms of its opposition to in-house administrative law judges at the Securities and Exchange Commission (SEC). In early 2018, it argued for the president's power to remove such officials, in the case of *Lucia v. SEC*. "The president's constitutional responsibility to faithfully execute the laws requires adequate authority to remove subordinate officers," Solicitor General Noel Francisco told the court in February 2018. Francisco argued,

> The framers understood the close connection between the president's ability to discharge his responsibilities as head of the executive branch and his control over its personnel ... The president's ability to execute the law is thus inextricably linked to his authority to hold his subordinates accountable for their conduct.

In June 2018, the Supreme Court agreed that the internal SEC judges should be under the president's control.

Some of Trump's signing statements suggest that he might endorse the idea of departmentalism, which is popular among unitarians and holds the three federal branches are (co)equal and therefore equally have the right to make constitutional judgments. In February 2017, Trump policy advisor Stephen Miller spoke about court decisions against Trump's executive order on immigration and refugees and disparaged the idea of judicial supremacy, according to which the Supreme Court has the last word on constitutional interpretation:

> we've heard a lot of talk about how all the branches of government are equal. That's the point. They are equal. There's no such thing as judicial supremacy. What the judges did, both at the ninth and at the district level was to take power for themselves that belongs squarely in the hands of the president of the United States.

Another aspect of Trump's presidency that suggests a unitary-like assertion of equal constitutional judgment viz. the judiciary concerns the Deferred Action for Childhood Arrivals (DACA) program. Trump ended DACA ostensibly because he believed that the Obama policy was not constitutional. As Keith Whittington noted, "Only Congress had the authority to alter the immigration status of the aliens who fell under the scope of DACA. It would exceed presidential authority to unilaterally grant an 'executive amnesty' in response to congressional inaction." Nevertheless, "the

Trump administration asserted an independent constitutional judgment that DACA was inconsistent with the administration's understanding of its own constitutional responsibilities."

Criticisms of Trump as Unitary

Criticism of alleged presidential excess from partisan opponents is to be expected, so it is not surprising that Democrats articulated various criticisms of Trump's unitarian proclivities. For example, pornographer Larry Flynt, who offered $10 million for information that would lead to Trump's impeachment, said "Trump has proven he's dangerously unfit to exercise the extreme power accrued by our 'unitary executive.'" But Trump's unitary-like actions have also come in for criticism by a variety of academics. And even some conservative proponents of the unitary executive have said that Trump has gone too far. For example, John Yoo proclaimed his concern about this in a *New York Times* op-ed in February 2017, saying "even I have grave concerns about Mr. Trump's uses of presidential power."

Conclusion

This chapter has examined the unitary executive in the twenty-first century, with a focus on its dramatic revival under George W. Bush. On balance, thus far Trump's presidency has been more unitary than that of Barack Obama, Bill Clinton, or George H.W. Bush, though not as avowedly unitarian as those of Reagan or George W. Bush. It is striking that the unitary presidency has been as pronounced as it has been under Trump, given that Trump's political party controlled all three branches of the federal government and a majority of state governorships during his first two years in office. The fact that the unitary executive was so prominent so early for Trump under those circumstances is therefore a telling indicator of the priority of this approach to the presidency. And there is reason to believe that it could well increase under the Democratic House majority. Despite its many controversies, ambiguities, and uncertainties, the unitary executive appears to be alive and well in 2019.

4

NORMATIVE ASSESSMENT OF THE UNITARY EXECUTIVE

The previous three chapters discussed the unitary executive theory and how it has played out across 23 decades and 45 presidencies. Regardless of whether one happens to agree with or approve of a particular unitary action by a particular president, or even of a general type of unitary action used by different presidents at different times, there is the broader question of whether one might agree with the theory of the unitary executive overall. On balance, is it a theory that deserves support and acceptance or criticism and rejection?

This chapter will briefly evaluate some of the main normative arguments for the unitary executive: it will consider whether the unitary executive is faithful to the wishes of the American founders, consonant with (or even mandated by) the Constitution, justified in terms of necessity or the doctrine of inherent power, facilitates good governance and administrative efficacy, and fosters accountability. Not every unitarian would endorse every one of these arguments, and there are various other arguments that one might make for the unitary executive, but these are among the most common and important ones. As we will see, in each of these regards the evidence is mixed, or least there are enough mitigating considerations or counterarguments that are plausible or persuasive enough that overall the normative case for the unitarian executive remains contentious or problematic.

The Founders

A primary argument in favor of the unitary executive theory is that it supposedly reflects the intentions of America's founders. The founders are greatly revered, and many people would agree that their views should be valued above others, so aligning a political project with the founders is an effective way to make it compelling. Unitarians often claim that their view is precisely what the framers of the U.S. Constitution wanted, given widespread dissatisfaction with the inadequate provision of executive power under the Articles of Confederation and also the rejection of a multiple or plural executive at the 1787 Constitutional Convention.

Unitarians often point to James Wilson's remarks at the convention and especially to Alexander Hamilton in *Federalist* 70, as those sources speak of the utility of executive unity. According to Madison's convention notes, Wilson declared, "that unity in the Executive instead of being the fetus of Monarchy would be the best safeguard against tyranny." Similarly, in *Federalist* 70, which was published six months after the convention, Hamilton sought to rebut concerns about executive power. He wrote, "There is an idea, which is not without its advocates, that a vigorous executive is inconsistent with the genius of republican government." For Hamilton, this view was "destitute of foundation." For him, "Energy in the executive is a leading character in the definition of good government," and the first ingredient in energy is unity. Hamilton contended,

> That unity is conducive to energy will not be disputed. Decision, activity, secrecy, and despatch [sic] will generally characterize the proceedings of one man in a much more eminent degree than the proceedings of any greater number; and in proportion as the number is increased, these qualities will be diminished.

Hamilton also argued, "all multiplication of the executive is rather dangerous than friendly to liberty."

For unitarians, quotes like these demonstrate that the founders endorsed the unitary executive. Yet, there are several considerations that push back against that conclusion. For example, while unitarians tend to perceive *Federalist* 70 as an argument for why a single president might be better than a legislative group, it is really concerned with the advantages of a single executive over a plural executive; its claim is that a sole executive is preferable to a plural one, not that the sole executive is preferable to Congress. Indeed, in *Federalist* 70 Hamilton praises the abilities of Congress.

Moreover, while Hamilton certainly was an advocate of an energetic executive, Hamilton's writings do not envision an unchecked president. As Michael Genovese (2011, 136) points out, Hamilton's energetic executive is not without limits:

> If one reads Hamilton's comprehensive analysis of presidential power in *The Federalist Papers*, it is clear that his energetic executive is embedded in a system of countervailing and shared powers; his is not a presidency above or independent of the Congress or the rule of law.

Indeed, some of Hamilton's writings suggest a more nuanced view than the unitarian interpretation. For example, in *Federalist* 69 he writes,

> the executive authority, with few exceptions, is to be vested in a single magistrate. This will scarcely, however, be considered as a point upon which any comparison can be grounded; for if, in this particular, there be a resemblance to the king of Great Britain, there is not less a resemblance to the Grand Seignior, to the khan of Tartary, to the Man of the Seven Mountains, or to the governor of New York.

According to Vicki Divoll (2013, 150), this means "Hamilton was saying that vesting the executive power in one person does not confer power in and of itself. The president's power comes from other sources in Article II – not the Vesting Clause." Similarly, in *Federalist* 77 Hamilton wrote that the president should share the removal power with the Senate: "the consent of that body would be necessary to displace as well as to appoint."

Beyond the matter of nuance in Hamilton's views, Hamilton was just one of the founders; he was just one of the 55 delegates who attended the convention. Casual claims about what "the framers" or "the founders" believed should be met with skepticism, as the founders held a variety of views, some of which do not support the idea of a unitary executive. For example, Edmund Randolph believed that the proposed new executive would be far too strong. As James Madison's convention notes from June 1, 1787 indicate:

> Mr. Randolph strenuously opposed a unity in the Executive magistracy. He regarded it as the foetus of monarchy. We had he said no motive to be governed by the British Government as our prototype ... the fixed genius of the people of America required a different form of Government. He could not see why the great requisites for

the Executive department, vigor, despatch and responsibility could not be found in three men, as well as in one man. The Executive ought to be independent. It ought therefore in order to support its independence to consist of more than one.

Madison himself expressed views that do not comport with the unitary view. In *Federalist* 47, Madison disavowed the view that the three "departments ought to have no partial agency in, or no control over, the acts of each other," which he saw as a misinterpretation of Montesquieu. And in *Federalist* 49 Madison wrote, "The several departments being perfectly co-ordinate by the terms of their common commission, none of them, it is evident, can pretend to an exclusive or superior right of settling the boundaries between their respective powers." This suggests that the president does not have the sole authority to determine what executive power entails.

Furthermore, the above discussion of the founders' views glosses over distinctions that can be very important. Facile invocations of the founders or the framers tend to elide significant differences among related but distinct groups: should we focus on the group of people who led the American Revolution, or those who composed or signed the Declaration of Independence (with its litany of complaints about the excesses of the British monarch), the Articles of Confederation (with its virtual lack of any executive power), or the U.S. Constitution? What about those who ratified the Constitution and thereby brought it into effect? Good arguments can be made for excluding or prioritizing any of those groups. And insofar as one might be inclined to take a generous interpretation and to include a broad range of those individuals in the set whose views are to be privileged, then the degree of diversity of course grows, making it very difficult to discern any one coherent view about the propriety of the unitary executive.

The Constitution

Aside from what the American founders thought about the unitary executive, there is the issue of what the U.S. Constitution actually says about it. Unitarians assert that the theory of the unitary executive is consonant with, or even mandated by the constitutional text. Yet, the term "unitary executive" does not appear in the Constitution. That might not be surprising, since the explicit unitary executive theory was not named until the 1980s. Regardless, unitarians often point to several parts of the Constitution to support the theory.

In particular, the grant of executive power in Article II is clearly different from the grant of legislative power that precedes it. Article I begins with the pronouncement that "All legislative powers herein granted shall be vested in a Congress," while Article II begins, "The executive power shall be vested in a President." It seems unlikely that the difference was due to carelessness by the constitutional drafters, so the claim that the difference is intentional and therefore important is compelling. For unitarians, Article II's reference to "the executive power," with a definite article and without Article II's limitation of "herein granted," indicates an unlimited grant of power.

Writing in *Pacificus* 1 (on June 29, 1793), Hamilton argued that the different constitutional language about legislative and executive powers indicates that the president was given a "general grant" or a "comprehensive grant" of executive power:

> The second Article of the Constitution of the UStates, section 1st, establishes this general Proposition, That "The Executive Power shall be vested in a President of the United States of America." The same article in a succeeding Section proceeds to designate particular cases of Executive Power ... It would not consist with the rules of sound construction to consider this enumeration of particular authorities as derogating from the more comprehensive grant contained in the general clause, further than as it may be coupled with express restrictions or qualifications; as in regard to the cooperation of the Senate in the appointment of Officers and the making of treaties; which are qualifications of the general executive powers of appointing officers and making treaties: Because the difficulty of a complete and perfect specification of all the cases of Executive authority would naturally dictate the use of general terms – and would render it improbable that a specification of certain particulars was design[e]d as a substitute for those terms, when antecedently used. The different mode of expression employed in the constitution in regard to the two powers the Legislative and the Executive serves to confirm this inference. In the article which grants the legislative powers of the Government, the expressions are – "All Legislative powers herein granted shall be vested in a Congress of the UStates"; in that which grants the Executive Power the expressions are, as already quoted "The Executive Power shall be vested in a President of the UStates of America." The enumeration ought rather therefore to be considered as intended by way of greater caution, to specify and regulate the principal articles implied in the definition of Executive Power; leaving the rest to flow from the

general grant of that power, interpreted in conformity to other parts of the constitution and to the principles of free government. The general doctrine then of our constitution is, that the Executive Power of the Nation is vested in the President; subject only to the exceptions and qualifications which are expressed in the instrument ... This mode of construing the Constitution has indeed been recognized by Congress in formal acts, upon full consideration and debate ...

In short, for Hamilton the different language of Articles I and II indicates a broad grant of executive power, notwithstanding the brief list of particular powers in Article II.

Historian Forrest McDonald (1994, 181) offers a similar interpretation of the Constitution's treatment of executive power:

> The more general vesting in Article 2, combined with the specification of certain presidential functions and duties, presupposes that 'executive power' had an agreed-upon meaning. Given the delegates' knowledge of the subject from history, political philosophy, and experience, it seems evident that some of them, at least, thought of executive power as contingent and discretionary: the power to act unilaterally in circumstances in which the safety or the wellbeing of the republic is imperiled; power corresponding to that of ancient Roman dictators, or to Bracton's gubernaculum, or to Fortescue's dominium regale; power, in sum, that extends beyond the ordinary rules prescribed by the Constitution and the laws.

The above interpretations about broad executive power are certainly plausible. But the constitutional text is vague and open to other interpretations that are less favorable to the unitarian position. For example, Lessig and Sunstein (1994, 40) claim,

> The framers meant to constitutionalize just some of what we now think of as 'the executive power,' leaving the balance to Congress as it thought proper. What follows from this is that if there were some functions that were not within the domain of what the framers were constitutionally vesting in the President when they vested 'the executive power,' then there are some functions over which the President need not, consistent with the original design, have plenary executive control.

Moreover, it is by no means clear that the two words "herein granted" are really sufficient to ground the entire unitarian project and to justify all that unitarians claim. As David Alvis et al. (10) put it, "the vesting clause is a thin reed on which to place so much weight." Surely if the founders really intended to constitutionalize the unitary executive, the Constitution would more clearly do so.

Some unitarians therefore turn to other parts of Article II to buttress their interpretation. For example, some point to the "take care" clause, which directs the president to ensure that laws are faithfully executed, arguing that it gives the president personal control over all executive decision-making, especially when read in conjunction with the vesting clause. As Todd Tatelman (2010, 9) explains, for some unitarians the President's constitutional duty to "take care that the Laws be faithfully executed" could not be fulfilled if the Vesting Clause were not "a substantive grant of executive power to the President." But the combination of the vesting and "take care" clauses to produce what unitarians want is controversial and open to various other interpretations. It seems equally plausible that the "take care" clause merely gives the president a sort of supervisory power over some subordinates' decisions, rather than complete control over all ostensibly executive activities.

Additionally or alternatively, some unitarians point to the presidential oath of office as a constitutional warrant for broad executive power. Article II contains this oath that an individual must take in order to become president: "I do solemnly swear (or affirm) that I will faithfully execute the Office of President of the United States, and will to the best of my Ability, preserve, protect and defend the Constitution of the United States." Some see the oath as permitting the president to make his own determinations about matters of constitutionality and how best to safeguard the government, as many unitarians advocate. For others, however, the oath commits the president to obey (rather than supersede) the rule of law and the limits of the Constitution.

Thus, unitarians invoke various parts of Article II to argue that the unitary executive theory is consonant with or even required by the Constitution. But as noted above, those textual claims are open to objections. And beyond what the constitutional text says, there is the issue of its historical background. To claim that the founders wanted all executive power placed in one person's hands is perhaps to put too much weight on the frustrations of dealing with the likes of Daniel Shays under the Articles of Confederation and to put too little weight on the frustrations of dealing with an unaccountable monarch before the Articles.

Beyond the question of whether certain constitutional clauses might accord the president broad powers, the Constitution is also unclear about many of the specific powers and practices that unitarians promote. For example, the Constitution does not explicitly give the president the power to remove officials, to manage the regulatory process, to control information, or to issue signing statements. The Constitution does not specifically preclude such actions, but neither does it specifically provide for them.

Aside from what the Constitution may say about executive power, there is also the issue of what it says about Congress and its relation to the executive branch. Contrary to the unitary executive theory, the Constitution gives Congress virtually unlimited power to control the executive. Section 8 of Article I lists many specific things that "Congress shall have power" to do, then it concludes with this broad grant of authority: "To make all Laws which shall be necessary and proper for carrying into Execution the foregoing Powers, and all other Powers vested by this Constitution in the Government of the United States, or in any Department or Officer thereof." And Article II says that while the president may appoint officers, "Congress may by law vest the appointment of such inferior officers, as they think proper, in the President alone, in the courts of law, or in the heads of departments." Thus, the Constitution explicitly gives Congress the power to structure the executive branch and to direct its departments and officers.

Less dramatically, as Heidi Kitrosser notes, "the Constitution permits Congress, acting through the legislative process, to accord the president less than complete control over all discretionary executive decisions and those who make them" (Kitrosser, 143). Thus, Congress could prevent the president from firing people without good cause, and it could "create zones of partial independence from presidential control within the executive branch" (Kitrosser, 144).

Ultimately, the Constitution does not clearly and convincingly provide for the unitary executive. Some aspects of it might accord with some unitarian claims, but others are in tension with the doctrine. This should not be a surprise, since the Constitution is not as much a coherent statement of a particular political principle as it was the result of various necessary compromises. On many topics, the Constitution does not so much speak clearly as it mumbles or gestures obliquely, and that seems to be the case with regard to the unitary executive.

One of the more significant statements about the ambiguity of the constitutional status of the unitary executive came from a senior member of Reagan's legal staff, Solicitor General Charles Fried. In his memoirs, Fried (1991) claimed that the unitary executive was less constitutionally compelling than unitarians argue and that it was "not literally compelled by the words of the Constitution. Nor did the framers' intent compel this view."

Originalism

Many of the preceding considerations are predicated on the assumption that if the original meaning of the Constitution could be discerned, then that meaning should prevail. In short, unitarian arguments about the constitutional text tend to be rooted in a commitment to the originalist mode of constitutional interpretation.

But originalism can be problematic. As philosopher Samuel Freeman (2018) has argued, originalism can refer either to the original meaning of the Constitution's terms or to how the people who wrote it or ratified it understood it at the time, and those different formulations can result in different interpretations. Furthermore, John Locke, who had perhaps the single greatest influence on the Constitution, argued against originalism of a sort, saying that people could not be bound by their ancestors. Moreover, says Freeman, the Constitution is ostensibly authored by "We the People," such that the relevant body for understanding the Constitution is arguably the people, including contemporary Americans.

Apart from whatever problems originalism might have, why should the originalist mode of interpretation be privileged over other alternatives? After all, originalism is only one way to interpret. People who believe that constitutional arrangements should or must be cognizant of contemporary realities are apt to care less about whether any particular constitutional point comports with the views of a few men in the 1780s. In other words, the argument goes, that was then and this is now; so long as some aspect of contemporary governance is not radically at odds with the Constitution, why should it be rejected out of hand in favor of some arbitrarily privileged alternative? The question of the best way to interpret the Constitution is enormously controversial. But the salient point here is that insofar as constitutional arguments for the unitary executive rely on originalism as the preferred mode of constitutional interpretation, those arguments may well fail to persuade people (not least of whom judges) who happen to have different interpretive preferences.

A further point about originalism is that it might actually argue against, rather than for, the unitary executive. Heidi Kitrosser makes this claim. As Mark Graber (2018) explains, Kitrosser

> points to framing evidence that the president was understood as merely responsible for ensuring that the persons charged by Congress with the responsibility for implementing policy were doing their jobs. The president is responsible for ensuring the post office delivers the mail, but Congress is free to specify how the mail will be delivered and who will report to Congress on whether the mail is

being delivered. This vision of the president as an overseer explains why Congress may command both the president and other executive branch officers to provide the national legislature with the information Congress needs to legislate and determine the effectiveness of existing legislation.

As the discussion here has indicated, unitarians tend to favor originalism, but originalism can be problematic, it need not lead to unitarian conclusions, and it is but one way to interpret the Constitution. There is the related issue of who may interpret the Constitution, and on that point the unitarian argument may be more persuasive: despite the long and widespread acceptance of judicial review, presidents have at times asserted their own right to interpret the Constitution. Nothing in the Constitution specifically designates the Supreme Court as the sole authoritative interpreter, and unitarians tend to support presidential claims to have a legitimate role to play in constitutional interpretation.

Necessity and Inherent Power

At times, unitarians invoke necessity as a justification for what the unitary executive theory would support. In other words, even if the words of the Constitution do not clearly authorize a unitary executive or a particular unitary action, it might nevertheless be permissible on the grounds that it was or is necessary, perhaps for the survival or well-being of the regime. For example, Assistant Attorney General Jay Bybee's memo of August 1, 2002 about interrogation methods explicitly invoked the necessity defense, saying (39–41) "We believe that a defense of necessity could be raised, under the current circumstances, to an allegation of a Section 2340A violation," regarding the ban on torture in title 18 of the United States Code.

The so-called "argument from necessity" has some historical pedigree, as Jefferson arguably invoked it regarding the Louisiana Purchase, as did Lincoln regarding the Civil War, and FDR threatened to act according to it. Richard Nixon appeared to invoke it when he told David Frost in 1977: "in war time, a president does have certain extraordinary powers which would make acts that would otherwise be unlawful, lawful if undertaken for the purpose of preserving the nation and the Constitution." Lincoln's articulation of the point is perhaps the most familiar:

> Are all the laws but one to go unexecuted and the government itself go to pieces lest that one be violated? Even in such a case, would not

the official oath be broken, if the government should be overthrown, when it was believed that disregarding the single law, would tend to preserve it?

Many people find Lincoln's rhetorical question persuasive, and political theorists from John Locke to Harvey Mansfield have articulated similar rationales for an executive acting beyond or even contrary to the letter of the law. However, the argument from necessity is not unassailable. As Genovese (2011, 158) has pointed out, even if the argument from necessity is convincing, that does not make it constitutional; "while 'necessity' is a powerful argument, it is not a constitutional argument."

Additionally, although these considerations are perhaps more relevant to the empirical considerations in the next chapter, there are historical and jurisprudential reasons for resisting the argument from necessity. For example, despite his invocation of the argument from necessity, Lincoln asked Congress to authorize his wartime suspension of the writ of habeas corpus, as if he knew that necessity alone was insufficient to justify his action and that traditional legislative permission was required. Similarly, Jefferson sought retroactive congressional acceptance for the Louisiana Purchase – a sort of ex post facto permission slip, as if one were needed. If the president actually believed that he had the expansive powers that some adherents of the unitary executive theory postulate, then congressional acceptance would be unnecessary, so the fact that presidents have at times sought the latter suggests that they believed they did not possess the former.

The judiciary has also cast doubt on the viability of the argument from necessity. In the Civil War case of *Ex parte Milligan* (1866), Justice David Davis's majority opinion basically rejected the argument from necessity:

> No doctrine involving more pernicious consequences was ever invented by the wit of man than that any of its provisions can be suspended during any of the great exigencies of government. Such a doctrine leads directly to anarchy or despotism, but the theory of necessity on which it is based is false; for the government, with the Constitution, has all the powers granted to it, which are necessary to preserve its existence.

Similarly, in *Hamdan v. Rumsfeld* (2006), the Court's majority opinion indicated that "exigency alone" cannot justify unconstitutional actions. Exigency is perhaps a slightly different argument than necessity, but it is close enough that *Hamdan* and *Milligan* may both go against the argument from necessity.

Closely related to the consideration of necessity is the idea that the president possesses inherent power. And in George W. Bush's version of the unitary executive (though not in other versions), the idea of inherent power was often prominent. For some unitarians, the idea of inherent executive power can be an attractive alternative, and a functional equivalent, to an expansive reading of Article II or a claim of necessity.

But the idea of inherent executive power is very controversial, even among unitarians. For example, Steven Calabresi and Christopher Yoo (2008, 419) contend that the unitary executive does not also justify inherent executive powers: "the historical record does not support claims that the unitary executive is the source of broad, inherent executive power." According to Julian Ku (2010, 615), inherent power and the unitary executive are separate issues, as "there is no necessary correlation between unitary executive power theory and inherent executive power." And that is not necessarily a bad thing for some unitarians, since the doctrine of inherent power is problematic. For example, Louis Fisher (2010, 569) argues that the idea of inherent presidential power is incompatible with the Constitution. Other commentators contend that the case of *In re Neagle* (1890) might indicate that the Court was prepared to accept some inherent presidential power, but the salient point here is that there is no real consensus on inherent power, and as a result any version of the unitary executive that rests on inherent power is especially controversial.

Administrative Efficacy

Apart from the question of its constitutionality, proponents of the unitary executive theory often claim that it is good for administrative efficacy and governance. This claim tends to take several different forms. First, as Justice Antonin Scalia said in his dissent in *Morrison*, "It is … an … advantage of the unitary Executive that it can achieve a more uniform application of the law." In other words, a unitary executive supposedly ensures that laws are carried out and enforced in the same way, whereas a non-unitary executive would presumably entail unequal execution of the law.

Second, some argue that the unitary executive can be good for democratic politics in that it can ensure that collective action problems do not prevent democratic preferences from being enacted. Congress is infamously adept at using its oversight and appropriations roles to impose on public policy the unrepresentative interests and priorities of certain individual members, whereas the president is supposedly a national steward who can rise above narrow interests to ensure that the true national interest is served, or at least that the will of large congressional majorities is not thwarted. In short, insofar as the president is (more) representative of most Americans' preferences than Congress, it may be appropriate that he has more power to administer the machinery of government. As Christopher Yoo (2010, 248) says, the unitary executive ensures "that administrative policy reflects majority preferences."

A third form of the pro-unitarian argument for administrative efficacy holds that in order for a president to effectively be in charge, to control administration, and to execute the law, he must be able to control, and if necessary remove, people below him. In short, the president needs to be able to hold his subordinates accountable. As James Madison said in 1789 during the first Congress, "I conceive that, if any power whatsoever is in its nature executive it is the power of appointing, inspecting and controlling those who execute the laws."

The argument is essentially that the unitary executive facilitates a clear chain of command, with subordinates dutifully carrying out the decisions of the chief executive. If it were otherwise, and if underlings had a wide scope of individual decision-making, then presumably the process of administration would be more cumbersome and potentially problematic. This view is perhaps similar to Thomas Hobbes's argument in *Leviathan* that anything less than completely unified authority will inevitably lead to conflict.

Unitarian arguments about administrative efficiency may take other forms, but those noted above are typical. And on some level they may be persuasive. However, they are not unassailable. For example, the fair application of a law does not necessarily require that the application always be by the same individual. And while the president may be able to rise above the parochial political interests of individual Members of Congress, his own political prospects are subject to the well-known distorting effects of the Electoral College.

Furthermore, the arguments for administrative efficacy tend to ignore and in fact to run contrary to another administrative value, namely stability. Stability is undoubtedly a principal value in good governance, yet the unitary executive might go against it. Under a truly unitary executive who can impose his will on the bureaucracy, public policy could change radically with a change in the presidency (even more so that it presently does). As Stephen Skowronek (2009, 2100) says:

> When the notion of a presidential stewardship is stripped of progressive provisions for collective oversight by the nation's *prudentes*, when the notion of a politicized bureaucracy is stripped of Jacksonian provisions

for collective oversight by the party, when the notion of a concert of power is stripped of Jeffersonian provisions for collective oversight by Congress – when the extra-constitutional ballast for presidential government is all stripped away and the idea is formalized as fundamental law, the original value of stability in government is all but lost from view.

Accountability

Another main argument in favor of the unitary executive is accountability. The unitary executive arguably ensures that the president is responsible, so that the public can hold him accountable and support him or not as his administrative record merits. The unitary executive fosters accountability by rendering the president answerable and enabling voters to register their approval or disapproval.

Hamilton is one source for this point. As Hamilton wrote in *Federalist* 70: "It often becomes impossible, amidst mutual accusations, to determine on whom the blame or punishment of a pernicious measure ... ought to fall." As Reagan's Attorney General Edwin Meese told the Federal Bar Association in 1985, "The men who wrote the Constitution were keenly concerned with accountability," and "excessive agency independence serves to defeat accountability in government." And Todd Tatelman (2010, 9) articulates the argument about accountability as follows: "dividing executive authority among multiple governmental entities decreases the general public's ability to hold executive officials accountable, can increase administrative bargaining costs, and may lead to debilitating collective action problems." In *Free Enterprise Fund v. Public Company Accounting Oversight Board* (2010), the Court appeared to endorse the accountability argument of unitarians, as it criticized the law's limitation on the removal power "for good cause shown," saying,

> [t]he diffusion of power carries with it a diffusion of accountability ... Without a clear and effective chain of command, the public cannot determine on whom the blame or the punishment of a pernicious measure, or series of pernicious measures ought really to fall.

The argument for accountability has its appeal, but even if one is inclined to place a high value on accountability, that does not necessarily mean that one should support the unitary executive. For example, legal scholar Heidi Kitrosser (2015) has argued that rather than foster accountability, the unitary executive may in fact undermine it. Her argument has two features (regarding information and neutrality), and it turns on a distinction between formal and substantive neutrality. As Mark Graber (2018) explains the distinction:

> Proponents of formal accountability emphasize public capacity to remove officials whom popular majorities conclude are not performing their duties. Officials are constitutionally accountable when they stand for regular election. Substantive accountability … requires that the public has the information necessary to make an intelligent decision on whether public officials should be accountable. Under this framework, officials are constitutionally accountable when their actions and the justifications for their actions are known to the public.

Moreover, Kitrosser argues that this distinction is not just some semantic nicety, but that the founders cared about substantive as well as formal accountability. She claims (152),

> Accountability indeed was a central preoccupation of the founders. Yet their concerns extended beyond the ballot box mechanisms of formal accountability. Beyond those essential mechanisms, the founders assumed the need for myriad means to ensure the information flow necessary to add substance to formal accountability.

Kitrosser claims that the unitary executive can hurt substantive accountability because it can inhibit the flow of information, as when it promotes secrecy and keeps information from the public. For example, under a unitary executive, the White House may use OMB "to alter or suppress information – whether in the form of reports, testimony, proposed rules or rulemaking records – that agencies were otherwise prepared to make public" (189). Similarly, she says, "unfettered presidential control can be used, for example, to keep truthful information from emerging from the executive branch through White House vetting of congressional testimony, pressure to alter scientific findings for political reasons, or secretive influence over agency policy decisions" (144).

The other type of substantive accountability that the unitary executive can inhibit concerns neutrality. Some unitarians say that an unelected bureaucracy should be overseen by someone who is elected, and they contend that anything short of presidential control accords some role to unelected bureaucrats, such that advocates of democracy should favor the unitary executive. However, presidential control may well politicize things that should perhaps not be political. For some, bureaucratic independence, neutrality, and expertise and legitimate values that should be respected and fostered. As Kitrosser (191–192) notes, "studies in the political science literature support the intuition that excessive politicization has costs for agency competence and expertise." If the president staffs the bureaucracy with ideological loyalists who ensure that his views prevail over those of career public servants, uses handpicked White House czars instead of congressionally approved officials to manage public policy, or forces agencies to do his bidding in when it comes to rulemaking, those practices may well render bureaucratic outcomes suspect. With the sort of influences and interference that the unitary executive provides, citizens are apt to question whether regulations are the result of political considerations rather than sound science or sensible public administration.

Kitrosser is not alone in making these sorts of arguments. For example, Skowronek (2076–2077) says,

> even in its most modest forms, the theory undercuts administrative arrangements designed to secure the independence of prosecutors, regulators, accountants, forecasters, personnel officers, scientists, and the like. It discounts the notion of objective, disinterested administration in service to the government as a whole and advances in its place the ideal of an administration run in strict accordance with the President's priorities.

Similarly, Richard Ellis (458–489) has noted that even if the unitary executive fosters responsiveness, "critics of the doctrine place at least equal weight on the value of neutral competence, that is, professional norms of impartiality, codes of best practices, and legal and scientific expertise."

Conclusion

This chapter has briefly discussed and assessed several different arguments in favor of the unitary executive theory. Altogether, some of the arguments are more persuasive than others, but each is open to various objections and counterarguments, and none is so radically compelling as to settle the debate or conclusively prove the desirability of the unitary executive. As a result, the unitary executive remains attractive for some but not for others. While this chapter has been examined normative claims about whether the unitary executive *should* exist, the next chapter will examine empirical claims about whether it *does* in fact exist.

5

EMPIRICAL ASSESSMENT OF THE UNITARY EXECUTIVE

This chapter seeks to build on the evaluative discussion of the preceding chapter by asking whether the unitary executive – regardless of what its normative merits and shortcomings might be – is empirically accurate. Apart from one's normative views about it, is the unitary executive a conception that maps well onto reality? Does the unitary executive theory accurately describe what really happens in the White House and within the executive branch, or is actual practice more complicated than the abstract principle?

In order to explore this issue, it might be useful first to consider a basic conceptual distinction drawn from analytic philosophy: is the unitary executive a metaphysical possibility, and (if so) is it an ontological reality? In other words, could it be possible for the unitary executive actually to exist, or is it an impossibility; and insofar as its existence is hypothetically possible, does it happen to exist or not? On both counts, there are compelling arguments on both sides.

Could the Unitary Executive Exist?

Before assessing whether the unitary executive actually exists, one might first ask if it could possibly exist, and some considerations suggest that it could not. As Christopher Yoo (2010, 247) explains,

> A number of commentators observe that it is impossible for any one person to exercise control over a bureaucracy as large as the federal

government's. In such a world, a unitary executive, in which the president exercises meaningful control over all aspects of the administration, remains a practical impossibility.

Similarly, Patrick O'Brien (2017, 174) points to

> the problem of feasibility – specifically, the fact that it is simply not credible to expect presidents, one after the next, to maintain complete control over the executive branch … even in cases when the president has complete legal control over executive operations, his actual control is necessarily incomplete.

And Louis Fisher (2010, 591) claims,

> The Constitution does not empower the President to carry out the law. That would be an impossible assignment. It empowers the President to see that the law is faithfully carried out. The great bulk of that work is done by Executive Branch employees who remain legitimately outside the President's direct control provided they faithfully discharge their assigned tasks.

Considerations from organizational theory and business also suggest that the unitary executive might be a practical impossibility. For example, as O'Brien (174) notes, the Nobel Prize-winning economist Herbert Simon pointed out that large organizations seldom if ever exhibit true top-down rational administrative behavior, and unity of command conflicts with the many internal specializations that characterize most large organizations.

The reaction to major financial regulatory requirements in the twenty-first century suggests a similar point. The Sarbanes-Oxley Act of 2002, which was passed in response to the collapse of Enron and WorldCom and sought to combat fraud and ensure the financial health of public corporations, required corporate executives to personally certify the accuracy of financial statements. And rules promulgated to implement the Dodd-Frank Act of 2010, which was passed in response to the financial crisis of 2008 and sought to protect consumers, required the CEO of a credit rating agency (CRA) annually to certify that the firm's controls and procedures were effective and that its ratings were accurate. For both laws, business leaders complained that it was difficult, if not impossible, to fully comply with such requirements, as the top executive simply could not vouch for every little thing the entire company did.

What is true of major businesses may also be true of the executive branch: it can be hard for the chief executive to be truly responsible for everything that occurs under his command. The fact that the executive branch has so many people and groups doing so many different things therefore suggests that no one person could really direct it all.

These types of concerns call into question the practical feasibility of the unitary executive theory, but they do not altogether demonstrate that it would be impossible. For some unitarians, even if day-to-day management falls short of complete knowledge and control, as long as the president is able to direct subordinates when he wants and to fire them when they come up short, the executive branch would still be meaningfully unitarian. And insofar as the unitary executive could possibly exist, it now remains to determine whether it does in fact actually exist.

Does the Unitary Executive Actually Exist?

As Vicki Divoll (2013, 148) has said, "It has been called the 'Unitary Executive Theory' for a reason – it is just a theory … it is not a doctrine, it is not a law, it is nothing but an intellectual discussion." Divoll's point is provocative, but insofar as multiple presidential administrations and judicial opinions have explicitly invoked the unitary executive, it is not just a fiction. Furthermore, it is clearly the case that a presidential administration very much reflects the character and desires of the president, and it is also true that the president wields considerable control over the executive branch. But is the executive branch actually unitary in practice? The following considerations offer mixed evidence.

Court Cases

Insofar as the practice of judicial review since *Marbury v. Madison* (1803) makes the U.S. Supreme Court the sole authoritative interpreter of the Constitution, it makes sense to consider how the Court has ruled on unitary issues. Although the unitary executive theory has not been the explicit subject of extensive jurisprudence, the term "unitary executive" has occurred in the opinions of the federal judiciary multiple times. And as we have seen in the previous chapters, various cases have addressed the unitary executive in some fashion. A few examples indicate that the judiciary has not clearly endorsed the unitary executive.

In *Marbury v. Madison*, the Court touched on several points that are central to debates about the unitary executive. For example, it noted that the president "is authorized to appoint certain officers, who act by his authority and in conformity with his orders," as if to support the view that the president may control his subordinates via his orders. However, *Marbury* also touched on the question of the president's removal power and indicated that it was not absolute:

> Where an officer is removable at the will of the Executive, the circumstance which completes his appointment is of no concern, because the act is at any time revocable, and the commission may be arrested if still in the office. But when the officer is not removable at the will of the Executive, the appointment is not revocable, and cannot be annulled. It has conferred legal rights which cannot be resumed.

Thus, the Court in *Marbury* gestured at a limit on the presidential removal power, but it did not elaborate on the matter. The Court also made a rough distinction between official duties that were ministerial and hence governed by legal and institutional constraints and those that were more discretionary and hence governed by the desires of the president. Subsequent cases echoed this distinction.

In *Kendall v. United States* (1838), the Court upheld the president's removal power but also found that Congress could create executive officials with ministerial tasks beyond the control of the president. As Krent (2008, 552) explains the opinion, "The Court reasoned that, particularly in light of the 'ministerial' nature of the act in question, the President had no power to second-guess the Postmaster's determination." The Court said that if it were to recognize a presidential power to change the determinations of subordinates, that "would be clothing the President with a power entirely to control the legislation of Congress," which would be unconstitutional. *Kendall* also largely rejected the idea that the "take care" clause gives the president a "dispensing power" that would permit him "entirely to control the legislation of Congress and paralyze the administration of justice."

In *Myers v. United States* (1926), Chief Justice (and former President) William Howard Taft wrote the majority opinion, in which he articulated a robust defense of the president's removal power. Unitarians tend to cite *Myers* as defending a broad presidential power to remove subordinates, but Taft's opinion did note some areas in which a president's power to control, change, or influence executive officials' determinations was limited, even if the president's power to fire the officials was not.

In *Humphrey's Executor v. United States* (1935), the Court made a distinction between administrative officials who had executive powers and those who had duties that were in some sense judicial or legislative. For the latter group, Congress could place limits on the president's power of removal. Thus, just nine years after *Myers*, the Court unanimously approved of Congress's ability to limit the president's right to fire executive officials in independent agencies whose functions are in some sense quasi-legislative or quasi-judicial.

One year later, in *United States v. Curtiss-Wright Export Corp.* (1936), the Court found that the president possessed broad independent constitutional powers in the realm of foreign affairs, and Justice Sutherland spoke of the president as the nation's "sole organ" in foreign affairs. However, some commentators (e.g., Fisher 2017) have noted that Sutherland's "sole organ" claim was just dicta or nonbinding. Furthermore, it was arguably based on a misreading of a speech that John Marshall made in the House in 1800. According to Fisher (2010, 570–571), "Marshall meant that after the two branches had decided national policy, either by statute or by treaty, it was the President's duty to inform other nations of our policy and to execute the law." And Sutherland's mention of the president as "sole organ" of international relations is followed in the very same sentence by the qualification that it is a power "which, of course, like every other governmental power, must be exercised in subordination to the applicable provisions of the Constitution." Additionally, the Court pushed back on the *Curtiss-Wright* view in *Zivotofsky v. Kerry* (2015). In short, Sutherland's characterization does not establish what unitarians claim.

In *Morrison v. Olson* (1988), the Court ruled 7-1 that the independent counsel provided for by the 1978 Ethics in Government Act was constitutional, as the law did not "unduly interfere" with the executive branch. This was a crushing blow for unitarians, as it validated a congressionally mandated judicial function within the executive branch that was not under the control of the president. Indeed, the Court in *Morrison* explicitly rejected some unitarian arguments, and as we have seen, some scholars contend that it effectively rejected the entire unitary executive theory. However, the fact that Scalia's unitarian dissent continues to resonate three decades later suggests that the issues of *Morrison* are not altogether settled.

Beyond the impact of any individual case, there is the matter of jurisprudence that extends across multiple cases and centuries. As discussed above, multiple cases have discerned different types of officials within the executive branch and found that some of them are at least partially shielded from the president's removal power. As Pierce (2010, 598) observes, "None of those cases has been overruled." Similarly, Elena Kagan (2001, 2326) predicted,

> the cases sustaining restrictions on the President's removal authority, whether or not justified, are almost certain to remain the law (at least in broad terms, if not in specifics); as a result, any serious attempt to engage the actual practice of presidential-agency relations must incorporate these holdings and their broader implications as part of its framework.

Altogether, while the Court has not directly ruled on the unitary executive theory, it has rejected elements of it on multiple occasions, and its de facto endorsements of aspects of it are limited.

Oaths to the Constitution, not the President

The unitary executive theory holds that the president essentially controls and can direct everyone and everything in the executive branch. But there are formal considerations that indicate the president's control is not complete. It is not true that everyone within the executive branch is accountable only to the president, as the Attorney General, the Federal Bureau of Investigation, and the Department of Justice, among others, all have other responsibilities.

Executive branch officers take an oath to support the Constitution, not the president. Other than the president alone, anyone elected or appointed to the federal civil service or the seven uniformed services (i.e., the five branches of the military, the U.S. Public Health Service Commissioned Corps, or the National Oceanic and Atmospheric Administration) must take an oath to "support the Constitution of the United States against all enemies, foreign and domestic; that I will bear true faith and allegiance to the same" per 5 U.S.C. 3331. These hundreds of thousands of employees pledge to support the entire system of government, not just the chief executive or whatever his or her preferences are.

Even within the strictures of military discipline, the Commander in Chief cannot command complete and unquestioned obedience by his subordinates. Even though people in the military take a version of the previous oath that includes the stipulation, "I will obey the orders of the President," it is illegal for a soldier to obey an order that he or she knows to be unlawful. The military's manual for courts-martial says:

> It is a defense to any offense that the accused was acting pursuant to orders unless the accused knew the orders to be unlawful or a person

of ordinary sense and understanding would have known the orders to be unlawful ..."

And the Uniform Code of Military Justice (UCMJ) indicates that members of the military have an obligation to disobey unlawful orders.

The Vice Presidency

If the unitary executive really existed, then it would presumably obtain especially at the highest levels of the executive branch, like those nearest to the president, such as the Vice President. After all, if a president cannot control his handpicked second-in-command, then complete presidential control of the vast executive branch is plainly implausible. Yet, vice presidents have at times exhibited independence from, and even opposition to, the presidents under whom they have served, even after the Twelfth Amendment removed the awkward scenario of the president and vice president being adversaries. For example, in 1825–1832, Vice President John Calhoun utilized the vice president's position in the Senate to stymie some of the legislative preferences of the two presidents under whom he served. More recently, in 2012 Joe Biden contradicted the Obama administration's stated policy on same-sex marriage when he announced his support for it on the television program "Meet the Press," leading Obama advisor Valerie Jarrett to accuse him of "downright disloyalty."

Beyond contradicting the president's policy preferences, the vice president might actively resist presidential decrees. For example, in 2007 Dick Cheney claimed to be a member of the legislative branch rather than the executive branch, as if his position were not under the control of the chief executive. Cheney made the claim in the course of arguing that he was not covered by an executive order, signed by George W. Bush himself, about safeguarding classified information.

The Legislative Veto

The use of a legislative veto is strongly at odds with the unitary executive. Ever since the 1930s, the legislative veto has enabled Congress to assert control over executive branch activities, by voting – in subcommittees, committees, or either or both chambers – to approve or disapprove of how the executive branch used powers that Congress had delegated to it. After the Court declared the unicameral version of the legislative veto unconstitutional in *INS v. Chadha* (1983), the practice of the House or Senate formally voting on such matters ended, but the legislative veto continues to the current day at the level of subcommittees and committees. Thus, even several decades after *Chadha*, executive agencies regularly accept congressional review of many of their activities. As Fisher (2010, 580–1) argues, "It would be difficult to find a clearer repudiation of the unitary executive model than the practice of congressional committees and subcommittees sharing with executive agencies certain administrative decisions."

Independent Agencies

Ever since the Brownlow Committee of 1937, unitarians have complained about independent agencies and the president's limited control of them, so the persistence of these agencies indicates that the executive branch is not thoroughly unitary. Starting with the Interstate Commerce Commission (ICC) in 1887, dozens of independent agencies have been created within the executive branch. Each of these agencies was created by Congress to perform specific tasks, and they are an essential feature of modern governance. Examples include the Federal Reserve Board, the Peace Corps, and a veritable alphabet soup of important agencies, such as the CIA, EPA, SEC, FTC, FCC, NLRB, SBA, NASA, and FEMA, among others. Many of these were established during the New Deal, and some like the Atomic Energy Commission or USIA were terminated or merged into other entities, but new ones have been created in recent times, like the Consumer Financial Protection Bureau of 2011. If the unitary executive were an accurate description of the executive branch, and if presidents consistently and jealously guarded against encroachments on their control, then presidents would have resisted the creation of each of these agencies and would have fought to end those whose creation they could not forestall. That simply has not occurred. To be sure, at times presidents have had their differences with some of these agencies, but presidents have been a party to the creation of these entities and have lived with them since the 1880s.

History & Laws

Beyond the above considerations about court cases, oaths, the vice presidency, the legislative veto, and independent agencies, there are various other historical considerations that also call into question the empirical validity of the unitary executive. Indeed, although Steven Calabresi and Christopher Yoo claim that presidents have consistently endorsed the unitary executive and resisted measures that are contrary to it, the historical record is mixed.

For example, the first Congress rejected a strict separation of powers amendment which had been included by James Madison in the original draft of the Bill of Rights. Although Congress appeared to believe that such an amendment was unnecessary, its rejection might nevertheless lend credence to the view that an overly stringent separation was undesirable, such that some legislative influence in the executive branch might well be constitutional.

Also in the first Congress, a careful examination of the so-called *Decision of 1789* suggests that Congress did not clearly endorse a robust constitutional removal power for the president, contrary to the claims of unitarians. In reality, Congress was very closely divided regarding the *Decision of 1789* and debated the matter for several weeks, with one legislative hurdle requiring Vice President John Adams to cast a tie-breaking vote. The episode did not so much reflect a clear and definitive legislative acceptance of a unitary presidential removal power as it reflected the lack of a clear consensus about the issue. As law professor Jerry Mashaw (2010) has written, the First Congress "seems to have had no fixed general idea about the relationship of the President to administration." And although Alexander Hamilton, John Marshall, and William Howard Taft all claimed that the *Decision of 1789* showed that Congress had endorsed the view that the president's removal power was based on Article II's grant of executive power, Louis Brandeis, Edwin Corwin, and others contend that a majority of Congress did not support that view. Thus, like many points that are adduced in favor of the unitary executive, the *Decision of 1789* is probably best seen as equivocal rather than determinative.

One might also look to administrative legal opinions that relate to the claims of the unitary executive. While the Attorney General and OLC were instrumental in the push for the unitary executive for Reagan and George W. Bush, at times the president's legal advisors have articulated far more reserved views about unitary actions. As Louis Fisher (2010, 577) notes, "On many occasions, an Attorney General has told the President that the White House has no *legal* right to interfere with administrative decisions." For example, Fisher points to an official opinion of the Attorney General from 1864 which said that "Neither the President nor a department head could 'revise and correct all the acts of his subordinates.'"

There are a great many laws whose provisions in one way or another differ from what the unitary executive theory holds, in that they place limits on what a president may do. For example, in the nineteenth century, the Tenure of Office Act did this, though Johnson resisted it. In the early twentieth century, Congress voted to place various limits on

Theodore Roosevelt's ability to issue certain types of executive orders and proclamations. In 1944, the Russell amendment stipulated that any agency established by executive order would require congressional assent for funding after its first year in existence. The Administrative Procedures Act (APA) of 1946 forbids "ex parte" contacts in the formal adjudicatory and rulemaking proceedings of federal regulatory agencies, so presidential interference with independent regulatory commissions can be legally and politically problematic. For example, in 1958 Eisenhower's close aide Sherman Adams was forced to resign when it became clear that he had intervened in regulatory matters before the Civil Aeronautics Board, the FTC, and the SEC.

Several of the major post-Watergate laws of the 1970s – the 1973 War Powers Act, the 1978 FISA, and the 1978 Ethics in Government Act – contain provisions that run contrary to the unitary executive. Laws like these indicate that many presidents have lived with limits on what the theory of the unitary executive would endorse. Some presidents have resisted or even ignored some of these laws, but they are laws nevertheless, and when presidents have violated them it has often been at considerable legal and political cost.

George W. Bush's avowedly unitary presidency offers another example of actual practice differing from unitarian principles. While some point to Bush's removal of nine U.S. Attorneys in 2006 as evidence of an attempt to assert unitary control, Fisher (2010, 584) suggests that the details of the episode show the opposite, in that "Repeated congressional hearings … could not locate in these firings any explicit actions or decisions by Bush, Attorney General Alberto Gonzales, or any other top officials." Karl Rove appeared to have played a central role in the firings, but there was no evidence that it flowed from the chief executive, as the unitary executive theory would suggest. In a 358-page report issued by the Department of Justice in September 2008, blame was dispersed, but insofar as any individual was singled out it was not the president but rather Kyle Sampson, who served as Chief of Staff to the Attorney General.

Scholars of unilateral presidential directives like executive orders are increasingly aware that unilateral tools do not necessarily indicate unitary control of the executive branch. For example, such directives are often issued only after extensive consultation with executive branch officials. Additionally, as Andrew Rudalevige (2012) has demonstrated, sometimes executive orders are resisted by executive officials after they are issued. As Kenneth Mayer (1999, 448) puts it "presidents cannot (and do not) issue one order after another and expect immediate and unquestioned obedience."

While the above considerations demonstrate respects in which the unitary executive has historically not been an accurate characterization of the presidency, a more charitable view is that the degree of presidential control has varied. Patrick O'Brien (2017, 182) argues that sometimes presidents have been able to restructure the administrative system and implement their own preferences, in a manner consistent with the unitary executive theory, but at other times presidential efforts have not resulted in success. But O'Brien (175) contends that even when the unitary executive should be most pronounced and effective – such as in the early nineteenth century, when the administrative system was much less complex – there is evidence of a lack of presidential control, as seen in Thomas Jefferson's inability to thwart the first central Bank of the United States. Based on such shortcomings, O'Brien argues, "the unitary executive framework is often a less-than-effective analytical tool for studying the presidency and policy making even for cases in which theoretically it should be the most effective, namely when the system of administration is relatively simple" (178).

Trump

The preceding section discussed a variety of historical considerations that question the empirical validity of the unitary executive. The current president offers more. Indeed, while there is much about the Trump presidency that is fairly unitary, there is also evidence that it is not altogether unitary. The following section considers some of the ways in which Trump falls short of a unitary executive.

Failure to Control

Despite Trump's boast in December 2017 that he had the "absolute right" to control the Department of Justice, he also publicly complained about his lack of control over it and also over the FBI. In November 2017 Trump said,

> You know, the saddest thing is that because I'm the president of the United States, I am not supposed to be involved with the Justice Department. I am not supposed to be involved with the F.B.I. I'm not supposed to be doing the kind of things that I would love to be doing. And I'm very frustrated by it.

Thus, by his own admission, Trump's degree of control falls short of what the unitary executive theory prescribes.

Another way in which Trump's rhetoric has indicated something less than a unitary executive concerns the so-called "deep state" against which the president and his advisors have often inveighed. For example, in May 2018, Trump claimed that a "criminal deep state" element planted a spy in his 2016 campaign. For Trump, the deep state is a group of people within government agencies who exercise influence or control apart from the desires of the president. For some, the "deep state" was responsible for embarrassing leaks to the media and may also account for Trump's desires not quickly leading to policy accomplishments, contrary to the dictates of the unitary presidency.

Another example of the lack of unitary control concerns Trump's first Attorney General, Jeff Sessions. Trump tried to prevent Sessions from recusing himself from the FBI's investigation of Russian influence in the 2016 election. Trump had his White House counsel, Donald McGahn, push Sessions to retain oversight of the inquiry. When Sessions nevertheless followed the Department of Justice's advice and recused himself in March 2017, Trump tried to get Sessions to reverse his recusal decision, but Sessions refused, despite the president's wishes.

Trump's apparent inability to end special counsel Robert Mueller's investigation is another example of how the unitary executive theory has failed in practice. As Jack Goldsmith (2018) notes,

> When Trump wanted Mueller gone [in summer 2017], he did not issue the order himself, as the unitary executive theory would suggest. He told White House Counsel Don McGahn to make it happen, but McGahn refused to ask the Justice Department to dismiss the special counsel, saying he would quit instead.

This episode indicates two respects in which Trump's experience failed to live up the unitary executive. First, Trump did not try to fire Sessions himself but asked an underling to do so. Second, the underling refused, and the president backed down.

In another example of the Department of Justice calling into question the accuracy of a strictly unitary executive, in June 2018 it agreed to give the House Intelligence Committee documents relating to its investigation of Hillary Clinton's unsecure e-mail usage while Secretary of State, after resisting doing so for months. Insofar as the control of information is a hallmark of the unitary executive, this concession by the executive branch is striking.

An Empty Executive

Presidents have long used their powers of nomination and appointment to enhance their control of the bureaucracy by staffing its upper echelons with loyalists who will do the president's bidding, and this form of control has grown over recent decades as the number of such appointees now reaches into the thousands. Yet, Trump was very slow to make many of these appointments, and many positions remained empty for a long time. Trump's failure to put in place hundreds of executive branch officials in a timely manner calls into question his commitment to a unitary executive. In other words, the power to control people seems meaningless if there is nobody there to control. (Alternatively, it might show that Trump believed he did not need a supporting cast.)

Inconsistency, not Unity

If the Trump administration were truly unitary, then the entire administration and indeed the entire executive branch would speak with one voice. But Trump's aides have often been caught off guard by presidential comments that undercut the views and policies that they were promoting. For example, in October 2017, Trump publicly undercut Secretary of State Rex Tillerson's efforts to negotiate with North Korea, saying via Twitter that Tillerson was "wasting his time trying to negotiate with Little Rocket Man." Trump also contradicted members of his Cabinet regarding border policy and the separation of migrant children from their families. These and other inconsistencies suggest that under Trump the executive branch is actually more splintered than it is unitary.

Subordinates' Support

Michael Wolf's 2018 book *Fire and Fury* contributed to the view that Trump might be unstable or not up to the job psychologically, and some commentators began to think about whether because of this incapacity the president might be removed via the 25th Amendment. Short of that radical remedy, others suggested that maybe the people of the West Wing could support the president or collectively render their incapable leader more capable. As columnist Ross Douthat wrote, "the big question is organizational, managerial, and psychological: Can the people who surround Donald Trump work around his incapacity successfully enough to keep his unfitness from producing a historic calamity?" That is essentially the opposite of the unitary executive: instead of the president imposing his will on the executive branch, executive branch officials impose their rationality on the president. The idea that a president's aides might help him is not novel, but a more strongly bottom-up model of aides holding the president's hand, guiding him, and helping him to do what he would be incapable of doing on his own is at odds with the traditional concept of a unitary executive.

Subordinates' Insubordination

At times, the words and deeds of officials in the executive branch have directly and purposely contradicted the president. In other words, the Trump presidency has arguably had instances of subordinates being openly insubordinate. The motivations of such subordinates vary, and their opposition has taken several different forms. People within the executive branch can resist the president by flatly refusing to implement his orders, by working very slowly or intentionally doing a poor job, providing leaks to the press, or speaking out publicly about their views. As Daniel Byman has argued, "Serving ... doesn't mean uncritical loyalty." But subordinates who do this resist risk incurring the president's ire or losing their jobs.

One way to assess this point is to consider how high-level officials in the Trump administration have responded to strong presidential pressure. For example, Jeff Sessions fought back, responding to Trump's criticisms and defending himself:

> As long as I am the Attorney General, I will continue to discharge my duties with integrity and honor, and this Department will continue to do its work in a fair and impartial manner according to the law and Constitution.

Rex Tillerson more directly rebutted Trump and his views, saying "The president speaks for himself." Similarly, H.R. McMaster repeatedly voiced strong criticisms of Russia's efforts to undermine American democracy, despite Trump repeatedly belittling McMaster's criticisms of Russia. When high-ranking subordinates rebut presidential assertions or articulate principled differences, the executive is not unitary.

There are other examples of this phenomenon. According to Byman,

> Defense Secretary Jim Mattis seems to have maintained his integrity while serving the president, pushing back against what he considered a flawed and risky approach to North Korea, slow-rolling

policies like Mr. Trump's proposed discharge of transgender troops, and otherwise using his influence and formal position to curb some of Mr. Trump's excesses.

Benjamin Wittes & Susan Hennessey note a couple other examples:

> After Trump seemingly called for police officers to rough up suspects during arrests, the acting head of the Drug Enforcement Administration, Chuck Rosenberg, circulated an email to agency staff condemning the remarks – an email that promptly leaked. Rosenberg did not display much concern for his continued employment prospects when he wrote that he had "an obligation to speak out when something is wrong." Even initially stalwart members of the administration like Director of the National Economic Council Gary Cohn are now publicly breaking ranks to condemn Trump. For a supposed tough guy, Trump is having a lot of trouble keeping his people in line.

In a related but even more dramatic way that officials have stood up to the president, Daniel Drezner has compiled a list of the dozens of times that Trump's aides have described him as a toddler.

For Bynam, effective pushback against Trump has also come from employees who chose to resign rather than stay and resist:

> if the president or a senior adviser has crossed an ethical line in another senior official's bailiwick, it is right for that official to leave – but not to do so silently. Walter Shaub Jr.'s criticisms of the president on ethics grounds and resignation as director of the Office of Government Ethics did far more to highlight the administration's ethical issues than if he had quietly taken another job.

Sometimes Trump's subordinates do not so much resist particular policies or pronouncements as they simply act as if the president did not exist at all. In other words, some executive officials have essentially ignored the president. This is true of some people in federal law enforcement. As journalist Peter Baker reported in November 2017, "investigators and prosecutors are so far ignoring the head of the executive branch in which they serve while military judges and juries are for the most part disregarding the opinions of their commander in chief." And as Goldsmith notes,

> What is most remarkable is the extent to which his senior officials act *as if Trump were not the chief executive*. Never has a president been

so regularly ignored or contradicted by his own officials. I'm not talking about so-called 'deep state' bureaucrats. I'm talking about senior officials in the Justice Department and the military and intelligence and foreign affairs agencies. And they are not just ignoring or contradicting him in private. They are doing so in public for all the world to see.

Given the various respects in which Trump's presidency has deviated from what the unitary executive theory would hold, some commentators have surmised that it is not so much unitary as anti-unitary. For example, Josh Blackman (2017) has argued that Trump is isolated within his own administration: "Rather than serving as a "unitary" executive, Trump is something of a "solitary executive," who is increasingly isolated within his own administration … As President Trump continues to isolate himself from his own cabinet, this executive branch can only grind to a painful halt." Yuval Levin articulates a similar point about the disconnect between Trump and the executive branch:

> when you talk to senior officials in this administration about their work, and when you listen to the ways they talk about it with journalists and activists, it's hard to avoid the conclusion that what we are seeing in the Trump era so far is the emergence of something like the inverse of the unitary executive. Today, the people who occupy executive-branch positions (in the White House and in other agencies) are all trying to administer the government as if there were a president in office directing their work in the ways presidents generally do, even as they know that isn't quite the case.

Similarly, Goldsmith says, "it's all a remarkable inversion of the unitary executive." And as Wittes and Hennessey put it, "The open insubordination of Trump's cabinet members is offensive to the very concept of the unitary executive … The Trump administration is the least unitary executive in modern presidential history."

Conclusion

Altogether, the points raised in this chapter indicate that the unitary executive often does not accurately depict the reality of the executive branch either historically or contemporarily. The president exercises considerable control over the executive branch, and at any point the presidency as an institution reflects the individual who is currently president, but complete unitary control remains elusive. In practice, the presidency is neither unitary nor non-unitary. The reality lies somewhere in the middle. The unitary executive theory is neither a fiction nor a fact. It partially exists and is partially absent. For its proponents it is an aspirational ideal that should be more fully realized; for its opponents it is a recurring aberration that will not altogether go away.

A Persistent Belief

Given the mixed empirical evidence for the unitary executive, one might ask why some people nevertheless persist in acting as if it did exist. If it is not altogether real, like a myth or a fairy tale, then why pretend it is? Is that not just a futile exercise in wishful thinking? In this regard, we might distinguish between the attitudes of academics and presidents themselves.

Academic Amenability

It may be the case that some scholars have a methodological proclivity to perceive a unitary executive even when it does not altogether exist. Specifically, methodological approaches to the study of the presidency that are beholden to rational choice theory may be predisposed to regard the unitary executive as real.

Rational choice scholarship on the presidency tends to highlight structural advantages that the president has as an individual over various other political entities. In such analyses, the president is generally depicted as immune to collective action problems, and perhaps possessing greater knowledge than other political actors and entities, such that he can easily act with dispatch as a "first mover." However, history arguably shows that presidents often do not in fact possess these advantages. As O'Brien argues (178), "the president's assumed structural advantages often fail to hold in practice."

It is a common criticism of rational choice that it does not capture or accurately model empirical reality. For example, in discussing the limits of rational choice, Terry Moe (710–711) concedes that "the players in these formal models are optimizers whose assumed capacities for calculation and information processing are typically light years beyond those of real people," and "its models ... tend to be overly simplified – meaning that they ... go too far in stripping away much of what is necessary to an adequate understanding." Despite that commendable awareness, however, some of Moe's own analysis is perhaps guilty of just such a shortcoming. For example, in 2014, David Lewis and Terry Moe claimed (383), "Presidents are not hobbled by collective action problems. Supreme within their own institutions, they can simply make authoritative decisions about what to do and then do it." The empirical evidence noted here very much calls into question the accuracy of such a characterization.

In short, viewing executive branch actions holistically – positing a rational individual instead of an inharmonious group – can facilitate calculations and models of rational decision-making and perhaps lend scholarship greater exactitude and predictability than it might otherwise be capable of, but that greater conceptual clarity may well come at the cost of not accurately capturing empirical reality.

This section has suggested some scholars' desire for clear explanations may render them inclined to see the unitary executive as real or complete even when it is not. Alternatively, it may well be the case that some scholars seem to like the unitary executive because some presidents seem to like the unitary executive.

Presidential Aspiration

Insofar as the unitary executive theory is more of a theory than a reality, why might a president nonetheless regard it as if it were real? For many political observers, presidents are motivated to want to accomplish many different things, yet they have relatively few good means towards those ends, and they are therefore inclined to latch onto tools, resources, and justifications that provide some measure of power or control. It is therefore perfectly natural and understandable that presidents have sought to exploit the ambiguities of the Constitution to their advantage. The unitary executive theory may well be an example of this phenomenon. It gives the president an ostensibly principled rationale or justification for doing what may be politically convenient to do. As the next chapter will discuss, politics of this sort may be central to the unitary executive theory.

CONCLUSION

Unitary Politics

The previous chapters have sought to explain what the unitary executive theory is, to explore its theoretical and constitutional bases, to examine its historical development from the founding era to the present day, and to consider normative and empirical arguments both for and against it. The discussion here has thus touched on a lot of complicated and controversial issues, many of which could be explored at greater length, but the intention has been to provide an accessible account of what the unitary executive theory is and why it matters. By way of a conclusion, this chapter focuses on the politics of the unitary executive. It is motivated by the view that the unitary executive is a fundamentally political theory and that many of the issues related to it are themselves fundamentally political.

Debates about whether the unitary executive comports with the founders' intentions, the constitutional text, historical and legal precedents, or the real world are all important, but what matters most is to what purposes these arguments are marshaled and how they are received. The arguments and evidence in favor of the unitary executive are equivocal. The unitary executive theory is not a magic wand or a panacea. It is not so well established or convincing or uncontroversial that a facile invocation of it will justify whatever a president wants to do in its name and silence his critics. The unitary executive theory practically invites controversy. Therefore, the question of whether or to what extent a president can utilize it is largely determined politically. The plausibility of a presidential invocation of the unitary executive theory depends crucially on why and how it is used. And the viability of the theory depends on the president's inclination to push the limits and on the institutional and public reaction to such action.

Politics

The political nature of the unitary executive theory may be seen by briefly considering the contexts in which it has been invoked and its rhetoric.

Particular Contexts

The unitary executive has clearly been political in its most prominent instantiations thus far: from its prototypical version under Richard Nixon, to its initial explicit formulation under Ronald Reagan, and its adaptation under George W. Bush.

As we have seen, even though the unitary executive theory as such did not exist until the 1980s, Nixon was very much a proto-unitarian or even the progenitor of the later unitary executive theory. Nixon's various efforts to assert greater control over the executive branch are generally known by the term the "administrative presidency," but they set crucial precedents that Reagan and others further developed under the unitary executive label. And Nixon's efforts in this regard were part of a strategy to do administratively what he could not accomplish with a united Democratic Congress and a recalcitrant bureaucracy. Nixon's use of administrative or unitary tactics was born of political necessity.

The creation of the explicit unitary executive doctrine in the 1980s was also thoroughly political. Promoted by a cadre of Reagan's legal advisors, the theory was consciously contrived to further conservative ends, to help halt the growth of government, and to turn the tide against the liberalism that had by and large dominated American politics for decades. Its proponents might have come to believe genuinely that the theory was an accurate portrayal of the founders' constitutional intentions, but its role as a tool of the conservative movement was its primary reason for being, and it was in service of those ends that it was promoted. It provided an ostensibly principled rationale for an ideological project.

The unitary executive theory attained its highest level of prominence and controversy under George W. Bush, who invoked it repeatedly and aggressively. For Bush, the unitary executive theory helped him to overcome the lack of a political mandate following the controversial election of 2000, to reinvigorate an office that some felt had been too weakened by post-Watergate reforms, and to shake off traditional limits in responding to the new exigencies of the war on terror. Regardless of which of those rationales one finds most compelling, Bush's use of the unitary executive theory was generally in the service of certain political ends.

Again, for each of the presidents for whom the unitary executive theory has been most prominent, its use has been driven by a political purpose, not just by considerations of routine governance or administration. The unitary executive theory served as the means toward the end of particular political projects. In short, the unitary executive theory has been a political tool, employed or marshaled for a nontrivial reason.

Partisanship and Ideology

Even if one is inclined to accept that the unitary executive theory is fundamentally political, that does not mean that it tracks traditional ideological or partisan divides. Thus far, all of the most explicitly unitary presidents have been conservative Republicans. But conservatives are not united in support of the unitary executive theory. For example, as Genovese (2011, 129) notes, George Will has decried it as a "monarchical doctrine." And Calabresi and Yoo have criticized Bush's version of it.

In principle, the unitary executive can be attractive to progressives, too. As we have seen, Democratic presidents (e.g., in recent decades, Carter, Clinton, and Obama) have at times acted in a unitary way. And an aggressive liberal president could use the unitary executive to promote egalitarianism and diversity, enhance the regulation of businesses, further environmental protections, or strengthen social welfare programs. In short, the unitary executive theory need not be associated only with conservative political projects.

General Contexts

Beyond the particular political contexts in which the unitary executive theory has been prominent, are there more general contexts that are conducive to the unitary executive theory? Political sympathy with the projects of the Reagan and George W. Bush administrations no doubt led some partisans to support their invocations of the unitary executive theory, but are there broader political circumstances that might be conducive to support for the unitary executive in general?

Perhaps persistent congressional dysfunction can render the unitary executive theory more likely to be invoked and also more acceptable once invoked. If the legislative process is blocked or Congress is intransigent, then alternative means may become politically palatable. Similarly, if executive officials seem to be officious, aloof, and unanswerable, or if bureaucratic action appears to be especially undemocratic or arbitrary, then the unitary executive may seem reasonable. Beyond those contexts, exigent circumstances may well be ripe for unitary responses. For example, war has generally led to greater deference to presidential desires, as Congress and the Courts have been less inclined to second-guess the chief executive in such times. Similarly, terrorism may well abet the unitary executive.

Even more generally, the political efficacy of the unitary executive depends on what the circumstances demand or may tolerate. Few Americans would ever want a truly weak executive, a mere figurehead. And many people like the sort of responsible chief executive suggested by Harry Truman's logo "the buck stops here." But no president is likely to enjoy being compared to Nixonian excesses like the 1973 "Saturday night massacre." Presidents must find a middle ground between appearing to be overly unitary or dictatorial and seeming to be insufficiently unitary or not in control.

Damaged Goods?

The previous sections discussed how different presidents have used the unitary executive theory for different purposes, but the unitary executive theory arguably is not constant – it has changed over the years, as have public perceptions of it. It is no longer a novel and untested theory; these days it comes with baggage. In particular, the unitary executive theory of today retains much of the controversy it acquired under George W. Bush. Bush's repeated and aggressive assertions of the unitary executive theory, and his extension of it to foreign policy and inherent powers, rendered the doctrine much more controversial than it had been in the late twentieth century.

This has two implications for the unitary executive theory today. First, contemporary invocations of the theory are likely to be more controversial and to elicit more criticism than was the case before Bush. The unitary executive theory now effectively comes with a warning label, indicating that great controversy is a common side effect of its use.

Second, it may be the case that Bush's radical view of the unitary executive rendered the more limited Reagan "classic" or traditional version more palatable in comparison, such that an invocation of the older version might now cause less blowback: a version of the unitary executive theory that is stripped of its Bushian connections to military action or inherent power, and perhaps invoked with less bravado, might well be less controversial. Indeed, Calabresi and Yoo's (2008) book essentially tried to redeem the unitary executive theory of the Reagan years, by showing how the earlier version differed from Bush's version. Both of these points suggest that a crucial aspect of the unitary executive theory today might be its rhetoric; it matters not just why or to what ends a president uses it, but also how he publicly defends its use.

Rhetoric

There has been considerable scholarly and political debate about whether or to what extent presidential words matter in terms of influencing public opinion, and there has been some scholarly work on the rhetoric of the unitary executive (e.g., Beasley 2010). But at present there seems to be no consensus among scholars of the presidency about whether or to what extent explicit rhetorical invocations of the unitary executive theory matter. There are different ways one might think about this issue.

An explicit invocation of the unitary executive theory can serve to explain or justify an action. Without an ostensibly principled rationale, a provocative presidential action may be more vulnerable to criticism, on the grounds that it is driven by convenience rather than by principle. Thus, there may well be a temptation for presidents to invoke the theory. Furthermore, invoking the theory to justify an action may also help to justify the theory itself, such that future invocations will be stronger. Repeated invocations may strengthen or at least normalize the theory, just by adding to the set of relevant precedents.

However, explicitly invoking the unitary executive theory may also bring unwanted controversy, by making acceptance of the action contingent on acceptance of the theory, which may itself be suspect. In that case, it might actually be better for the president not to invoke the theory. Additionally, for some presidents, if using the unitary executive theory entails being compared to Reagan or George W. Bush, then political considerations might push against using it.

But if a president acts pursuant to the unitary executive yet does not explicitly justify his action in terms of the theory, is his action any less unitary? If a president issues a signing statement that asserts his right to pass judgment on the constitutionality of the statute or indicates his inclination toward enforcing parts of it yet does not explicitly invoke the unitary executive theory as a justification, is the signing statement any less unitary? Must an opinion of the Attorney General or OLC or Solicitor General or a federal judge explicitly reference the unitary executive theory and quote chapter and verse from Hamilton in order to promote the unitary executive? For some, this may seem akin to Shakespearean ruminations about "a rose by any other name" or the question of whether a falling tree makes a sound if no one is there to hear it, but the explicit invocation of the theory may matter, in terms of whether it helps to justify both the action and the theory itself.

Since using the unitary executive theory entails some risk, are there not other ways for a president to do what he wants, without having to invoke the theory? For example, Obama at times acted in accordance with the theory but did not say as much. Moreover, while the theory of the unitary executive covers a variety of presidential actions, many of those actions might be justified in far less grandiose terms. Insofar as invocations of the unitary executive theory invite greater scrutiny or skepticism, a president might seek to defend a robust use of the removal power, executive privilege, or signing statements in other terms.

And short of boldly invoking the entire unitary executive theory, a president might instead draw on aspects of it. There are various resources that unitarians could utilize in the future: parts of Article II, Hamilton in *Federalist* 70, the Iran–Contra minority report, Meese's 1986 report, and certain court cases and opinions, including Taft's opinion in *Myers*, Southerland in *Curtiss-Wright*, Scalia's appellate opinion in *Bowsher*, Silberman's appellate opinion in *Morrison*, Scalia's dissent in *Morrison*, Yoo's memo of July 2001, and Thomas's dissents in *Hamdan* and *Hamdi*. Together, these and other texts put forth detailed and principled rationales for the unitary executive. Even if they did not enjoy prolonged victory or authority, they nevertheless remain resources that could be exploited in the future.

Temptation

Despite the difficulties that using the unitary executive theory can entail, the odds are that presidents will continue to use it. As Rozell and Sollenberger (51) note, "Once new powers are created or existing ones expanded, it is too tempting for a future president not to exercise them." Similarly, as Justice Robert Jackson wrote in his majority opinion in *Korematsu v. United States* (1944), when the Court validates an assertion of presidential power,

> The principle then lies about like a loaded weapon, ready for the hand of any authority that can bring forward a plausible claim of an urgent need. Every repetition imbeds that principle more deeply in our law and thinking and expands it to new purposes.

The theory of the unitary executive has not received judicial sanction, but despite its uncertain constitutional status, insofar as it has not been altogether discredited it is a resource that may be hard for presidents to resist.

Given the demands for the president to lead and to act, and given the relatively few and limited means a president has at his disposal, there is a strong temptation to latch on to a potentially powerful tool with some record of previous use, like the unitary executive theory. Again, the unitary executive theory has a decidedly controversial status and is by no means a universally acceptable and problem-free option. Far from it, the unitary executive is a highly contested conception with a mixed track record. Nevertheless, it can be an attractive option for some presidents in some circumstances.

Acquiescence or Resistance?

Regardless of how the president utilizes and promotes the unitary executive theory, its viability depends crucially on the acquiescence of the other branches. The efficacy of unitary executive theory as a governing tool requires not just that the president uses it, but also that political actors other than the president accede to it, or fail in their efforts to contest it. But what if they resisted effectively? Might not Congress, the courts, the executive branch, or the American people counter the unitary executive?

Congress

Although presidents and their advisors have been the main force behind the rise of the unitary executive, Congress has been complicit in it. This was particularly the case during George W. Bush's use of the unitary executive, perhaps because individual Members of Congress feared criticizing the president's actions in a time of national emergency (and high presidential approval ratings). Congress's de facto acquiescence to the unitary executive is striking in that Congress frequently spars with the president over public policy and governance and has the constitutional right to control aspects of the bureaucracy. Yet, Congress has largely accepted or even abetted the unitary executive, much as it has failed to counter the generations-long growth of presidential power and aggrandizement more generally.

Criticism of Congress is nothing new. Congress consistently has lower approval ratings than other parts of the U.S. political system, it often seems dysfunctional, and some scholars have even labeled it the "broken branch" of government. As unitarians are fond of pointing out, Congress is often beset by collective action problems of the sort that a single chief executive arguably is not. And its institutional problems are often exacerbated by partisan politics.

But Congress can on occasion be roused to do its job, to defend its constitutional prerogatives, and to resist executive excess. There have been periods in American history in which Congress has been the dominant branch. Congress need not – and from a constitutional perspective perhaps should not – acquiesce to the unitary executive. But how might Congress resist the unitary executive? Here, briefly stated, are some basic possibilities. Congress could legislate in greater detail, in order to narrow the scope for administrative maneuvering or variability in implementation. Congress could insert language into every bill in order to make it harder for a presidential signing statement to significantly alter or negate it. Congress could delegate less to the executive and maybe even undo previous delegations: if the executive branch is tasked with doing less, then there is less opportunity for it to do so in a unitary manner. Congress could use the de facto legislative veto more extensively than it currently does – though at the level of committees or subcommittees, per *INS v. Chadha* – so as to police how the executive implements the law. Congress could create more independent entities within the executive branch. Congress could use its power of oversight and investigation to reveal and critique what the executive branch does. And Congress could use its power of the purse to diminish the resources the president has at his disposal or even to defund much of the executive branch. Ultimately, Congress could vote to censure or impeach the president.

More generally, surely there is some way in which the individual and partisan motivations of Members of Congress could be marshaled to render the body collectively more capable of doing its constitutional due diligence. Partisan politics indicates that members of one political party have an incentive to call out executive excess when it comes from a president of the other party, and some Members' desire to rise within the ranks or to seek higher office might also incentivize greater scrutiny of the executive.

Along those lines, Congress could create a standing joint committee tasked with protecting its constitutional prerogatives and not ceding its authority up Pennsylvania Avenue to the White House; it could give an annual award (perhaps a variation on John F. Kennedy's "profiles in courage") to the Member who best defends it against executive encroachment; and it could give the minority party something closer to equal say and resources on its oversight committees, so as to permit partisanship to better police the executive. In short, there are various ways in which Congress might better resist the unitary executive.

However, the current prospects for more effective congressional resistance to the unitary executive are not promising. Routine political and electoral pressures are so strong that, short of a constitutional crisis or a major political scandal, it is hard to see how Congress as a body could be persuaded to exercise greater institutional vigilance.

The Courts

The judicial branch, and in particular the Supreme Court, is perhaps uniquely able to call out presidential excess and may therefore be a prime location for resistance to overzealous unitarianism. Landmark court decisions can set constitutional boundaries and make the president culpable for transgressions. However, the judiciary is also beset by certain limitations that may render it disinclined to boldly oppose executive excess. For example, the judiciary generally cannot enforce its views. As Hamilton wrote in *Federalist* 78: the judiciary has "neither force nor will, but merely judgment; and must ultimately depend upon the aid of the executive arm even for the efficacy of its judgments." Insofar as the judiciary relies on the executive branch to enforce its decisions, the judiciary may be especially reluctant to enlist the executive in curtailing the executive.

Additionally, there is the "political question" doctrine, which has long limited the ability or inclination of the judiciary to check some presidential practices. As Chief Justice John Marshall said in *Marbury v. Madison* (1803),

> The province of the courts is ... not to inquire how the executive, or executive officers, perform duties in which they have a discretion. Questions in their nature political, or which are, by the constitution and laws, submitted to the executive, can never be made in this court.

In practical terms, this means that federal courts have tried not to become involved in issues that are overtly political or that might be better resolved by the two more overtly political branches. For some, this judicial deference is part of the idea of judicial restraint, whereby the Court has or should have a principled disinclination to settle things that could be left to regular politics. In *Baker v. Carr* (1962), the Court explicitly formalized an approach to defining political questions and stipulated six criteria to help it flag political cases that should be avoided. Some thought the political question doctrine might decline after the Court's decision in *Bush v. Gore* (2000), but by all appearances it continues to limit the judiciary today.

Furthermore, as some academics have argued, even when the Court tries to curtail the executive, it can at times paradoxically enable the very things that it seeks to prohibit. In her assessment of attempts to curb executive power, Nancy Kassop (2011) notes that these efforts can end up legitimizing the executive practices that they are intended to limit, as the president can cleverly exploit the discretion that the rulings provide. Insofar as legal efforts to limit the executive can thus backfire, maybe the courts are wise not to try in the first place.

Despite these and other difficulties, the judiciary could still resist the unitary executive. It could strike down extreme unitary actions, uphold limits on the presidential removal power, safeguard the independence of some entities within the executive branch, limit the president's ability to control access to information, deprecate the significance of presidential signing statements, and declare that major anti-unitarian decisions like *Humphrey's Executor*, *Morrison*, and *Hamdan* are still binding.

At present, the prospects for the judiciary better resisting the unitary executive are not good. Consider the Court's 7-1 decision in *Morrison v. Olson* (1988), which refuted some unitarian claims and upheld the constitutionality of unitarians' *bête noire*, the special counsel. Ever since, unitarians have loathed *Morrison* and longed for its reversal. Indeed, Justice Antonin Scalia's lone unitarian dissent in *Morrison* has continued to attract attention over three decades after he issued it. In April 2018, several Senators cited Scalia's dissent in explaining their opposition to a bill to protect special counsel Robert Mueller. Senator Ben Sasse (R, NE) even said, "Many of us think we are bound" by Scalia's dissent. In 2015, Justice Elena Kagan called Scalia's dissent "one of the greatest dissents ever written and every year it gets better." And in 2016, two years before his confirmation to the Supreme Court, Judge Brett Kavanaugh said that he wanted to "put the final nail" in the coffin of *Morrison*. Several other current members of the Court (e.g., Alito) also appear hostile to *Morrison*, so if a similar case were to come before the Court today, unitarians might well get the result they desire.

The Executive Branch

Regardless of whether and how the other two branches could respond to the unitary executive, the reaction of people within the executive branch may be crucial. After all, it is the many individuals and entities within the executive branch who are most immediately affected by the unitary executive. Principled executive branch officials can stand up to presidential overreach by resisting it, openly criticizing it, or resigning in protest.

Attorney General John Ashcroft's dramatic hospital bed rejection of White House counsel Alberto Gonzalez's request to reauthorize a controversial domestic surveillance program in 2004 may be one example. And as we have seen, some executive officials have stood up to Trump and pushed back against some of his words and deeds, even when the president publicly belittled them. Ultimately, the Vice President and the Cabinet could resist the president and even initiate a process to remove him per 25th Amendment. Short of that radical step, executive branch officials do have a duty to support the Constitution, and many no doubt feel an obligation to support their particular office or agency, so that there may be good reasons for resisting when the president oversteps or seeks to personally control the entire executive branch.

The People

Apart from how politicians and public servants might respond to the unitary executive, a basic part of its acceptance or rejection is the reaction of the public. Even though many citizens may be unaware of the unitary executive theory per se, most people do at least have views about the individual who happens to be president, and journalistic accounts of particular political controversies tend to coalesce into well-known narratives of presidential action and power, such that the people may in fact have some general awareness of unitarian issues.

Even if a president can get away with doing something in the name of the unitary executive, in the sense that his action is not blocked or reversed, there may nevertheless be a political price for it. Arguably, this was what happened when Bill Clinton fired seven employees at the White House Travel Office in 1993, as it fed a growing narrative that the president was prepared to be heavy-handed in order to benefit his associates. Similarly, George W. Bush's many unitary actions supported the view that his was a stridently unilateral presidency. And Donald Trump's efforts to bend executive officials to his will have contributed to the popular perception that he is a bully or a would-be autocrat. Public perception that a particular presidential action fits a broader pattern of excess may thus serve as a political check on the unitary executive.

People who are familiar with the unitary executive may have a particular responsibility to scrutinize its invocation. At any point in time, many peoples' evaluations of the unitary executive theory tend to be driven largely by the extent to which it may further their own political preferences. But the unitary executive touches on such basic constitutional and governance issues that it should be of concern to all who value the American constitutional order, regardless of the narrow politics of the moment.

Presidents Themselves

Presidents themselves might also resist the unitary executive doctrine. As we have seen, presidents may have good reasons to embrace the unitary executive, but they may also have good reasons not to do so. The president might make a principled decision not to invoke the theory or even to criticize it, as Barack Obama arguably did. Such actions would probably not altogether discredit or render the theory unusable, but they might well increase the political costs for its use by future presidents.

And if the president decides to use or promote the unitary executive and play what law professor Mark Tushnet has called "constitutional hardball," then he must be prepared for the political cost of such actions. There may well be a political cost to his presidency, as discussed above. But there can also be institutional costs, to the presidential office and indeed to the health of the constitutional order. Unitarian assertions can cause constitutional crises and can also damage the norms and practices that make effective democratic governance possible. As Steven Levitsky and Daniel Ziblatt put it, "America's constitutional system ... requires forbearance. If our leaders deploy their legal prerogatives without restraint, it could bring severe dysfunction, and even constitutional crisis." Forbearance, or restraint in deploying powerful but controversial tools, is a trait that few might associate with the contemporary presidency, but it can be crucial. Not every individual president has placed a high value on the future well-functioning of the presidency as an institution, but some have, and some could and perhaps should be brought to do so.

The U.S. governmental system was designed to make it difficult to do things, and in that regard it has worked quite well over the years. American political history does contain instances in which a policy was enacted too hastily, in which hindsight suggests that something was done too easily or without sufficient care, but there are far more instances of inaction, when the system blocked action despite a majority desire to act. Therefore, there is a considerable temptation for the president (and others) to find a short-cut, to overcome the many divisions of power and the need for widespread agreement among different people and institutions. The unitary executive theory can be a tempting solution to the frustrations of regular politics.

But American democracy has survived and largely thrived for nearly two and one-third centuries with its system of divisions and checks and balances in place, despite the inefficiencies and frustrations that it can entail. That system and its traditions deserve our respect. The exigencies and conveniences of the moment should not blithely trump the wisdom of the founders or the balance and norms endorsed by the generations that followed them. Presidents owe it to themselves, their office, and their country to resist the facile fix, the easy but flawed and dangerous invocation of unitariness to cloak and excuse that which should perhaps not properly be. If and when the president sees fit to override such concerns and seeks to personally incorporate all powers of the federal government that might plausibly be seen as executive, then the rest of the constitutional system must endeavor to check him and to restore the proper balance.

EPILOGUE

While I was completing this book and seeing it through to publication in the winter of 2018–2019, nearly every day brought more news reports related to the themes of the book. But two events in particular underscored how significant and timely the unitary executive theory is.

First, in December 2018, the film *Vice* was released. *Vice* is a star-studded biopic about the rise to power of Vice President Dick Cheney, and it quickly met with critical and commercial success. The film contains a scene set in the mid-1970s in which Cheney (who was then deputy chief of staff for Gerald Ford) learns about the unitary executive theory from a young Antonin Scalia, planting the seed of what would decades later become the vigorously unitary presidency of George W. Bush. When Hollywood sees fit to dramatize a legal theory (albeit with some poetic license), it suggests that the theory is not just a subject for debates among academics but rather something of real significance for all people.

Second, in April 2019, special counsel Robert Mueller submitted his much-anticipated report about Russian meddling in the 2016 presidential U.S. election and whether Donald Trump had colluded with Russia or obstructed justice in trying to stymie the investigation. One of the report's findings was that on several occasions Trump had essentially tried to thwart the investigation, but his underlings repeatedly refused to carry out his orders, effectively saving the president from himself and demonstrating how various executive officials can check the chief executive's unitary aspirations, even in a very hierarchical administration.

Events such as these indicate that the unitary executive theory will continue to be important for the foreseeable future.

BIBLIOGRAPHY

Alvis, J. David, et al. *The Contested Removal Power, 1787–2010*. Lawrence: University Press of Kansas, 2013.

Bailey, Jeremy D. "The New Unitary Executive and Democratic Theory." *American Political Science Review*, Vol. 102, No. 4. (2008), pp. 453–465.

Baker, Peter. "'Very Frustrated' Trump Becomes Top Critic of Law Enforcement." *New York Times*. November 3, 2017.

Barber, Sotirios A. and James E. Fleming. "Constitutional Theory and the Future of the Unitary Executive." *Emory Law Journal*, Vol. 59 (2009), pp. 459–467.

Barber, Sotirios A. and James E. Fleming. "Constitutional Theory, the Unitary Executive, and the Rule of Law." *Nomos*, Vol. 50 (2011), pp. 156–166.

Barilleaux, Ryan J. and Christopher S. Kelley, eds. *The Unitary Executive and the Modern Presidency*. College Station: TAMU Press, 2010.

Barilleaux, Ryan J. and Jewerl Maxwell. "Has Barack Obama Embraced the Unitary Executive?" *PS: Political Science & Politics*, Vol. 50, No. 1 (2017), pp. 31–34.

Barr, William P. "Common Legislative Encroachments on Executive Branch Authority." 13 U.S. Op. Off. Legal Counsel, 248 (1989). (Memorandum from Assistant Attorney General, Office of Legal Counsel.) July 27, 1989.

Beasley, Vanessa B. "The Rhetorical Presidency Meets the Unitary Presidency." *Rhetoric & Public Affairs*, Vol. 13, No. 1 (2010), pp. 7–35.

Blackman, Josh. "The Solitary Executive." *Lawfare*. August 18, 2017.

Blumenstein, James F. "Regulatory Review by the Executive Office of the President." *Duke Law Journal*, Vol. 51, No. 3 (December, 2001), pp. 851–899.

Bradley, Curtis A. and Eric A. Posner. "Presidential Signing Statements and Executive Power." *Constitutional Commentary*, Vol. 23 (2006), pp. 307–364.

Burns, Sarah. "A New Model of Executive Power: A Montesquieuan Explanation of the Obama Presidency." *Perspectives on Politics*, Vol. 44, No. 4 (2015), pp. 247–256.

Bybee, Jay S. Memorandum for Alberto R. Gonzalez, Counsel to the President. Washington, DC: U.S. Department of Justice, Office of Legal Counsel. August 1, 2002.

Byman, Daniel. "Is It Possible to Serve Honorably in the Trump Administration?" *New York Times*. February 21, 2018.

Calabresi, Steven G. "Brett Kavanaugh and the Unitary Executive." *The Hill*. July 27, 2018.

Calabresi, Steven G. "Remove Morrison v. Olsen." *Vanderbilt Law Review*, Vol. 62 (2009), pp. 103–119.

Calabresi, Steven G. "Some Normative Arguments for the Unitary Executive." *Arkansas Law Review*, Vol. 48 (1995), pp. 23–104.

Calabresi, Steven G. "The President, the Supreme Court, and the Constitution." *Law and Contemporary Problems*, Vol. 61, No. 1 (Winter, 1998), pp. 61–82.

Calabresi, Steven G. "The Vesting Clauses as Power Grants." *Northwestern University Law. Review*, Vol. 88 (1994), pp. 1377–1405.

Calabresi, Steven G. and Joan L. Larsen. "One Person, One Office: Separation of Powers or Separation of Personnel?" *Cornell Law Review*, Vol. 79 (1994), pp. 1045–1157.

Calabresi, Steven G. and Gary Lawson. "The Unitary Executive, Jurisdiction Stripping, and the Hamdan Opinions: A Textualist Response to Justice Scalia." *Columbia Law Review*, Vol. 107, No. 4 (May 2007), pp. 1002–1047.

Calabresi, Steven G. and Daniel Lev. "The Legal Significance of Presidential Signing Statements." *The Forum*, Vol. 4, No. 2 (2006).

Calabresi, Steven G. and Saikrishna B. Prakash. "The President's Power to Execute the Laws." *Yale Law Journal*, Vol. 104 (1994), pp. 541–665.

Calabresi, Steven G. and Kevin H. Rhodes. "The Structural Constitution: Unitary Executive, Plural Judiciary." *Harvard Law Review*, Vol. 105 (April, 1992), pp. 1153–1216.

Calabresi, Steven G. and Nicholas Terrell. "The Fatally Flawed Theory of the Unbundled Executive." *University of Minnesota Law Review*, Vol. 93, No. 5 (2009), pp. 1696–1740.

Calabresi, Steven G. and Christopher S. Yoo. "The Unitary Executive during the First Half-Century." *Case Western Reserve Law Review*, Vol. 47 (1997), pp. 1451–1461.

Calabresi, Steven and Christopher S. Yoo. "The Unitary Executive in Historical Perspective." *Administrative and Regulatory News*, Vol. 31, No. 1 (2005), pp. 5–7, 13.

Calabresi, Steven G. and Christopher S. Yoo. *The Unitary Executive: Presidential Power from Washington to Bush*. New Haven, CT: Yale University Press, 2008.

Calabresi, Steven G. and Christopher S. Yoo. "The Unitary Executive during the Second Half-Century." *Harvard Journal of Law & Public Policy*, Vol. 26 (2003), pp. 667–801.

Calabresi, Steven G., Christopher S. Yoo, and Anthony Colangelo. "The Unitary Executive in the Modern Era." *Iowa Law Review*, Vol. 91 (2005), pp. 601–731.

Calabresi, Steven G., Christopher S. Yoo, and Laurence D. Nee. "The Unitary Executive during the Third Half-Century." *Notre Dame Law Review*, Vol. 80 (2004), p. 1.

Caminker, Evan. "The Unitary Executive and State Administration of Federal Law." *University of Kansas Law Review*, Vol. 45 (1997), pp. 1075–1112.

Carrington, Adam M. "To Inform and Recommend: Hamilton and the Constitutional Ground for Interaction Between Executive Officers and Congress." *Presidential Studies Quarterly*, Vol. 47, No. 4 (December, 2017), pp. 624–645.

Cash, Jordan T. "George Mason and the Ambiguity of Executive Power." *Presidential Studies Quarterly*, Vol. 48, No. 4 (October, 2018), pp. 741–767.

Coan, Andrew and Nicholas Bullard. "Judicial Capacity and Executive Power." *Virginia Law Review*, Vol. 102 (2016), pp. 765–831.

Coglianese, C. and Kristin Firth. "Separation of Powers Legitimacy: An Empirical Inquiry into Norms about Executive Power." *University of Pennsylvania Law Review*, Vol. 164 (2015), pp. 1869–1910.

Conan, Neil. "Exploring the Limits of Executive Power." NPR interview with Jeffrey Rosen and John Yoo. July 19, 2006.

Conley, Richard S. "The Harbinger of the Unitary Executive?" *Presidential Studies Quarterly*, Vol. 41, No. 3 (2011), pp. 546–569.

Corwin, Edward S. *The President: Office and Powers*. New York: NYU Press, 1940.

Corwin, Edward S. *The President's Removal Power under the Constitution*. New York: National Municipal League, 1927.

Cost, Jay. "Taming the Imperial Presidency." *National Review*. December 4, 2017.

Cross, Frank B. "The Surviving Significance of the Unitary Executive." *Houston Law Review*, Vol. 27 (1990), p. 599.

Crotty, William J. *Winning the Presidency, 2008*. New York: Routledge, 2015.

Crouch, Jeffrey, Mark J. Rozell, and Mitchell A. Sollenberger. "President Obama's Signing Statements and the Expansion of Executive Power." *Presidential Studies Quarterly*, Vol. 43, No. 4 (December, 2013), pp. 883–899.

Crouch, Jeffrey, Mark J. Rozell, and Mitchel A. Sollenberger. "The Unitary Executive Theory and President Donald J. Trump." *Presidential Studies Quarterly*, Vol. 47, No. 3 (September, 2017), pp. 561–573.

Currie, David P. "The Distribution of Powers after Bowsher." *Supreme Court Review*, Vol. 1986 (1986), pp. 19–40.

Dearborn, John A. "The Foundations of the Modern Presidency: Presidential Representation, the Unitary Executive Theory, and the Reorganization Act of 1939." *Presidential Studies Quarterly* (April, 2018), pp. 185–203.

Dellinger, Walter. "Re. The Constitutional Separation of Powers between the President and Congress." (Memorandum from Assistant Attorney General, Office of Legal Counsel.) May 7, 1996.

Devins, Neal. "Political Will and the Unitary Executive." *Cardozo Law Review*, Vol. 15 (1993–1994), pp. 273–312.

Divoll, Vicki. "Eight Things I Hate about the Unitary Executive Theory." *Vermont Law Review*, Vol. 38 (2013), pp. 147–154.

Douthat, Ross. "Trump's Petticoat Government." *New York Times*. January 6, 2018.

Drew, Elizabeth. "Power Grab." *New York Review of Books*. June 22, 2006.

Drezner, Daniel. "White House Aides Can't Stop Talking about President Trump Like He's a Toddler." *Washington Post*. April 21, 2017.

Driesen, David M. "Firing U.S. Attorneys: An Essay." *Administrative Law Review*, Vol. 60, No. 3 (Summer, 2008), pp. 707–727.

Eastland, Terry. *Energy in the Executive: The Case for the Strong Presidency.* New York: Free Press, 1992.

Elliott, E. Donald, et al. "Agency Autonomy and the Unitary Executive." *Washington University Law Quarterly*, Vol. 68 (1990), pp. 495–524.

Ellis, Richard J. *The Development of the American Presidency.* 2nd ed. New York: Routledge, 2015.

Ellis, Richard J. and Saikrishna Prakash. "Resolved, the Unitary Executive is a Myth." Chapter in Richard J. Ellis and Michael Nelson, eds., *Debating the Presidency: Conflicting Perspectives on the American Executive.* 3rd ed. Los Angeles, CA: CQ Press, 2014, pp. 16–37.

Engel, Steven A. "April 2018 Airstrikes against Syrian Chemical-Weapons Facilities." Memorandum Opinion for the Counsel to the President. May 31, 2018.

Epps, Garrett. "Constitutional Myth #3: The 'Unitary Executive' is a Dictator in War and Peace." *The Atlantic.* June 9, 2011.

Farina, Cynthia R. "False Comfort and Impossible Promises." *Journal of Constitutional Law*, Vol. 12, No. 2 (February, 2010), pp. 357–424.

Farina, Cynthia R. "Undoing the New Deal through the New Presidentialism." *Harvard Journal of Law & Public Policy*, Vol. 22 (1998), pp. 227–238.

Fisher, Louis. "Invoking Inherent Powers: A Primer." *Presidential Studies Quarterly*, Vol. 37, No. 1 (March, 2007), pp. 1–22.

Fisher, Louis. *Supreme Court Expansion of Presidential Power: Unconstitutional Leanings.* Lawrence: University Press of Kansas, 2017.

Fisher, Louis. "The Unitary Executive and Inherent Executive Power." *Journal of Constitutional Law*, Vol. 12, No. 2 (2010), pp. 569–591.

Fitts. Michael A. "The Paradox of Power in the Modern State." *University of Pennsylvania Law Review*, Vol. 144, No. 3 (1996), pp. 827–902.

Freeman, Samuel. "Interpreting the Constitution." 60-second Lecture, University of Pennsylvania. September 17, 2018. https://www.sas.upenn.edu/node/14170

Fried, Charles. *Order and Law: Arguing the Reagan Revolution – A Firsthand Account.* New York: Simon & Schuster, 1991.

GAO. "Presidential Signing Statements Accompanying the Fiscal Year 2006 Appropriations Act." June 18, 2007.

Gattuso, James. "The Rulemaking Process and Unitary Executive Theory." Testimony before the Subcommittee on Commercial and Administrative Law House Judiciary Committee. May 6, 2008.

Genovese, Michael A. *Presidential Prerogative: Imperial Power in an Age of Terrorism.* Stanford, CA: Stanford University Press, 2011.

Ginsburg, Douglas H. and Steven Menashi. "Nondelegation and the Unitary Executive." *Journal of Constitutional Law*, Vol. 12, No. 2 (2010), pp. 251–276.

Goldsmith, Jack. "Our Non-unitary Executive." *Lawfare.* July 30, 2017.

Goldsmith, Jack. *The Terror Presidency: Law and Limits inside the Bush Administration.* New York: Norton, 2007.

Graber, Mark. Review of Heidi Kitrosser, *Reclaiming Accountability.* Chicago, IL: University of Chicago Press, 2015. In *Law and Politics Book Review*, Vol. 28, No. 2 (April, 2018), pp. 19–22.

Green, Bruce A. and Rebecca Roiphe. "Can the President Control the Department of Justice?" *Alabama Law Review*, Vol. 70, No. 1 (2018), pp. 1–75.

Harrison, John. "The Unitary Executive and the Scope of Executive Power." *Yale Law Journal Forum*. January 24, 2017, pp. 374–380.

Hasian, Marouf, Jr. "Dangerous Supplements, Inventive Dissent, and Military Critiques of the Bush Administration's Unitary Executive Theories." *Presidential Studies Quarterly*, Vol. 37, No. 4 (2007), pp. 693–716.

Hollis-Brusky, Amanda. "Helping Ideas Have Consequences: Political and Intellectual Investment in the Unitary Executive Theory, 1981–2000." *Denver University Law Review*. Vol. 89, No. 1 (2011), pp. 197–244.

Horton, Scott. "Six Questions for Steven Calabresi, Author of 'The Unitary Executive.'" *Harper's*. September 30, 2008.

Jurecic, Quinta. "Body Double: What Medieval Executive Theory Tells Us about Trump's Twitter Accounts." *Lawfare*. April 24, 2017.

Kagan, Elena. "Presidential Administration." *Harvard Law Review*, Vol. 114 (2001), pp. 2245–2385.

Kassop, Nancy. "Reverse Effect: Congressional and Judicial Restraints on Presidential Power." Chapter in Meena Bose, ed., *President or King? Evaluating the Expansion of Executive Power from Abraham Lincoln to George W. Bush*. Hauppauge, NY: Nova, 2011, pp. 63–76.

Kelley, Christopher S. "'Faithfully Executing' and 'Taking Care' – The Unitary Executive and the Presidential Signing Statement." APSA Conference Paper, Boston, MA. 2002.

Kennedy, Joshua B. ""Do This! Do That!' and Nothing Will Happen" Executive Orders and Bureaucratic Responsiveness." *American Politics Research*, Vol. 43, No. 1 (2015), pp. 59–82.

Kitrosser, Heidi. *Reclaiming Accountability*. Chicago, IL: University of Chicago Press, 2015.

Kitrosser, Heidi. "The Accountable Executive." *University of Minnesota Law Review*, Vol. 93, No. 5 (2009), pp. 1741–1777.

Korte, Gregory. "Trump Issues Broad, 'Bush-style' Signing Statement on Spending Bill." *USA Today*. May 5, 2017.

Kovacs, Kathryn E. "Rules about Rulemaking and the Rise of the Unitary Executive." *Administrative Law Review*, Vol. 70, No. 3 (March, 2018), pp. 515–567.

Krent, Harold J. "Fragmenting the Unitary Executive." *Northwestern University Law Review*, Vol. 85 (1990), pp. 62–112.

Krent, Harold J. "From a Unitary to a Unilateral Presidency." *Boston University Law Review*, Vol. 88 (2008), pp. 523–559.

Krotoszynski, Ronald J., Jr. "The Unitary Executive and the Plural Judiciary: On the Potential Virtues of Decentralized Judicial Power." *Notre Dame Law Review*, Vol. 89 (2013–2014), p. 1021.

Ku, Julian G. "Unitary Executive Theory and Exclusive Presidential Powers." *Journal of Constitutional Law*, Vol. 12, No. 2 (2010), pp. 615–621.

Lessig, Lawrence. "Readings by Our Unitary Executive." *Cardozo Law Review*, Vol. 15 (1993), pp. 175–200.

Lessig, Lawrence and Cass R. Sunstein. "The President and the Administration." *Columbia Law Review*, Vol. 94 (1994), pp. 1–119.

Levin, Yuval. "The Supernumerary Executive." *National Review.* January 5, 2018.

Levitsky, Steven and Daniel Ziblatt. *How Democracies Die.* New York: Crown, 2018.

Lewis, David E. and Terry M. Moe. "The Presidency and the Bureaucracy: The Levers of Presidential Control." In Michael Nelson, ed., *The Presidency and the Political System.* Washington, DC: CQ Press, 2014, pp. 374–405.

Liberman, Lee S. "Morrison v. Olson: A Formalistic Perspective on Why the Court Was Wrong." 38 *American University Law Review,* Vol. 38 (1989), pp. 313–358.

Liebert, Hugh, et al., eds. *Executive Power in Theory and Practice.* New York: Palgrave Macmillan, 2012.

Lithwick, Dahlia. "Look for the Sign: The Fallout from President Bush's Signing-statement Spree." *Slate.* June 19, 2007.

MacKenzie, John P. *Absolute Power.* New York: Century Foundation Press, 2008.

McCarthy, Andrew C. "Trump and the Unitary Executive." *National Review.* April 12, 2018.

McDonald, Forrest. *The American Presidency: An Intellectual History.* Lawrence: University Press of Kansas, 1994.

Major, Mark. *The Unilateral Presidency and the News Media.* New York: Palgrave, 2014.

Mansfield, Harvey C., Jr. *Taming the Prince: The Ambivalence of Modern Executive Power.* New York: Free Press, 1989.

Markman, Stephen J. "Separation of Powers." April 30, 1986. (Executive memo commissioned by Attorney General Edwin Meese III.)

Marlowe, Melanie M. "The Unitary Executive." Chapter in Michael A. Genovese, ed., *Contending Approaches to the American Presidency.* Washington, DC: CQ Press, 2012.

Mashaw, Jerry L. "Center and Periphery in Antebellum Federal Administration: The Multiple Faces of Popular Control." *University of Pennsylvania Journal of Constitutional Law,* Vol. 12 (2010), pp. 331–356.

Mashaw, Jerry L. "Governmental Practice and Presidential Direction: Lessons from the Antebellum Republic?" *Willamette Law Review,* Vol. 45 (2009), pp. 659, 668.

Mayer, Jane. "The Hidden Power." *The New Yorker.* July 3, 2006.

Mayer, Kenneth. "Executive Orders and Presidential Power." *The Journal of Politics,* Vol. 61, No. 2 (May, 1999), pp. 445–466.

Mayer, Kenneth R. *With the Stroke of a Pen: Executive Orders and Presidential Power.* Princeton, NJ: Princeton University Press, 2001.

Miller, Geoffrey P. "Independent Agencies." *Supreme Court Review,* Vol. 1986 (1986), pp. 41–97.

Minority Report. House Select Committee to Investigate Covert Arms Transactions with Iran, Senate Select Committee on Secret Military Assistance to Iran and the Nicaraguan Opposition, 1987.

Moe, Terry. "The Revolution in Presidential Studies." *Presidency Studies Quarterly,* Vol. 39, No. 4 (December, 2009), pp. 701–724.

Moe, Terry M. and Scott A. Wilson. "Presidents and the Politics of Structure." *Law and Contemporary Problems,* Vol. 57, No. 2 (1994), pp. 1–44.

Moloney, K. and Samuel Krislov. "Legal-Administrative Responses and Democratic Deconsolidation." *Public Organization Review*, Vol. 16, No. 1 (2016), pp. 17–37.

Morris, Irwin L. *The American Presidency: An Analytical Approach*. New York: Cambridge University Press, 2010.

Nathan, Richard P. *The Administrative Presidency*. New York: Wiley, 1983.

Nathan, Richard P. *The Plot That Failed: Nixon and the Administrative Presidency*. New York: Wiley, 1975.

Nelson, Dana D. "The 'Unitary Executive' Question." *LA Times*. October 11, 2008.

Neustadt, Richard. *Presidential Power: The Politics of Leadership*. New York: John Wiley & Sons, 1960.

Nourse, Victoria. "Reclaiming the Constitutional Text from Originalism: The Case of Executive Power." *California Law Review*, Vol. 106 (February, 2018), pp. 1–44.

Nourse, Victoria. "The Special Counsel, *Morrison v. Olson*, and the Dangerous Implications of the Unitary Executive Theory." Issue Brief, American Constitution Society, June, 2018. https://www.acslaw.org/wp-content/uploads/2018/07/UnitaryExecutiveTheory.pdf

Nourse, Victoria F. and John P. Figura. "Toward a Representational Theory of the Executive." [Book Review of *The Unitary Executive*, by Steven Calabresi and Christopher Yoo, Yale University Press, 2008.]. *Boston University Law Review*, Vol. 91 (2011).

Nzelibe, Jide. "Does the Unitary Executive Really Need a Nationalist Justification?" *Journal of Constitutional Law*, Vol. 12, No. 2 (2010), pp. 623–636.

O'Brien, Patrick R. "A Theoretical Critique of the Unitary Executive Framework." *Presidential Studies Quarterly*, Vol. 47, No. 1 (2017), pp. 169–185.

Orentlicher, David. *Two Presidents are Better Than One*. New York: NYU Press, 2013.

Percival, Robert V. "Presidential Management of the Administrative State: The Not-So Unitary Executive." *Duke Law Journal*, Vol. 51, No. 3 (2001), pp. 963–1013.

Pierce, Richard, Jr. "Saving the Unitary Executive Theory from Those Who Would Distort and Abuse It." *Journal of Constitutional Law*, Vol. 12, No. 2 (2010), pp. 593–613.

Pildes, Richard H. "Law and the President." [Book Review of *The Executive Unbound*, by Eric Posner and Adrian Vermeule, Oxford University Press, 2010.] *Harvard Law Review*, Vol. 125 (2012).

Posner, Eric A. and Adrian Vermeule. *The Executive Unbound*. New York: Oxford University Press, 2011.

Prakash, Saikrishna Bangalore. *Imperial from the Beginning: The Constitution of the Original Executive*. New Haven, CT: Yale University Press, 2015.

Raffel, Burton. "Presidential Removal Power: The Role of the Supreme Court." *University of Miami Law Review*, Vol. 13 (1958), pp. 69–80.

Rogowski, Jon C. "Presidential Influence in an Era of Congressional Dominance." *American Political Science Review*, Vol. 110 (2016), pp. 325–341.

Roosevelt, Theodore. *An Autobiography.* New York: Macmillan, 1913.

Roosevelt, Theodore. Letter to George Otto Trevelyan. June 19, 1908.

Rosen, Jeffrey. "Power of One." *New Republic.* July 24, 2006.

Rosen, Jeffrey. "Uncle Sam." *New Republic.* January 30, 2006.

Rosenberg, Morton. "Congress's Prerogative Over Agencies and Agency Decisionmakers: The Rise and Demise of the Reagan Administration's Theory of the Unitary Executive." *George Washington Law Review,* Vol. 57 (1989), p. 627.

Rossiter, Clinton. *Constitutional Dictatorship.* Princeton, NJ: Princeton University Press, 1948.

Rozell, Mark J. and Mitchel A. Sollenberger. "The Unitary Executive Theory and the Bush Legacy." Chapter in Donald R. Kelley and Todd G. Shields, eds., *Taking the Measure: The Presidency of George W. Bush.* College Station: TAMU Press, 2013, pp. 36–54.

Rudalevige, Andrew. "Executive Branch Management and Presidential Unilateralism: Centralization and the Issuance of Executive Orders." *Congress & the Presidency,* Vol. 42 (2015), pp. 342–365.

Rudalevige, Andrew. "Executive Orders and Presidential Unilateralism." *Presidential Studies Quarterly,* Vol. 42 (March, 2012), pp. 138–160.

Sala, Richard K. "The Illusory Unitary Executive." *Vermont Law Review,* Vol. 38 (2013), pp. 155–197.

Savage, Charlie. "Bush Challenges Hundreds of Laws." *Boston Globe.* April 30, 2006.

Savage, Charlie. "Commanding Heights." *The Atlantic.* October, 2007.

Savage, Charlie. *Power Wars: The Relentless Rise of Presidential Authority and Secrecy.* Boston, MA: Back Bay Books, 2017.

Savage, Charlie. *Takeover: The Return of the Imperial Presidency and the Subversion of American Democracy.* New York: Little Brown, 2007.

Schlesinger, Arthur M., Jr. *The Imperial Presidency.* Boston, MA: Houghton Mifflin, 1973.

Schwartz, Frederick A.O., and Aziz Z. Huq. *Unchecked and Unbalanced: Presidential Power in a Time of Terror.* New York: The New Press, 2008.

Shane, Peter M. "Boundary Disputes: Jerry L. Mashaw's Anti-Formalism, Constitutional Interpretation and the Unitary Presidency." Chapter in Nicholas Parrillo, ed., *Administrative Law from the Inside Out.* Cambridge: Cambridge University Press, 2017, pp. 188–211.

Shane, Peter M. "Legislative Delegation, the Unitary Presidency, and the Legitimacy of the Administrative State." *Harvard Journal of Law and Public Policy,* Vol. 33, No. 1 (2010), pp. 103–110.

Shane, Peter M. *Madison's Nightmare.* Chicago, IL: University of Chicago Press, 2009.

Shane, Peter M. "The Originalist Myth of the Unitary Executive." *Journal of Constitutional Law,* Vol. 19 (2016), pp. 323–362.

Siemers, David J. "Imperial from the Beginning: The Constitution of the Original Executive." *Journal of American History,* Vol. 103, No. 2 (2016), pp. 459–460.

Skowronek, Stephen. "The Conservative Insurgency and Presidential Power: A Developmental Perspective." *Harvard Law Review,* Vol. 122, No. 8 (2009), pp. 2070–2103.

Sollenberger, Mitchel A. and Mark J. Rozell. *The President's Czars: Undermining Congress and the Constitution*. Lawrence: University Press of Kansas, 2012.

Somin, Ilya. "Rethinking the Unitary Executive." *Reason*. May 3, 2018.

Spitzer, Robert J. "Review of Reclaiming Accountability by Heidi Kitrosser." *Congress & the Presidency*, Vol. 42, No. 3 (2015), pp. 368–370.

Stiglitz, Edward H. "Unitary Innovations and Political Accountability." 99 *Cornell Law Review* (2014), pp. 1133–1184.

Strauss, Peter L. "Overseer, or 'The Decider?' The President in Administrative Law." *George Washington Law Review*, Vol. 75 (2007), p. 696.

Sunstein, Cass R. "The Myth of the Unitary Executive." *Administrative Law Journal*, Vol. 7 (1993), p. 299.

Tatalovich, Raymond and Steven E. Schier. *The Presidency and Political Science*. 2nd ed. New York: Routledge, 2014.

Tatelman, Todd B. "Supreme Court Nominee Elena Kagan: Presidential Authority and the Separation of Powers." Washington, DC: Congressional Research Service. June 4, 2010.

The University of Chicago Law School Faculty Blog. "What the 'Unitary Executive' Debate Is and Is Not About." August 6, 2007.

Thompson, William A.P., Jr. "Trump's Presidency: Transformative or Adhering to Rudiments of Executive Unitary Theory?" *CLIO*, Vol. 27, No. 2 (Summer, 2018).

Tillman, Seth Barrett and Michael D. Ramsey. "The Originalism Blog: An Exchange with Professor Michael Ramsey on the Unitary Executive." January 9, 2013. doi:10.2139/ssrn.2197209

Tushnet, Mark. "A Political Perspective on the Theory of the Unitary Executive." *Journal of Constitutional Law*, Vol. 12, No. 2 (2010), pp. 313–331.

Updegrove, Mark K. *The Last Republicans*. New York: Harper, 2017.

U.S. House Subcommittee on Commercial and Administrative Law. "Rulemaking Process and the Unitary Executive Theory." U.S. Government Printing Office. May 6, 2008.

Vaughn, Justin S. and Jose D. Villalobos. *Czars in the White House: The Rise of Policy Czars as Presidential Management Tools*. Ann Arbor: University of Michigan Press, 2015.

Waterman, Richard W. *Presidential Influence and the Administrative State*. Knoxville: University of Tennessee Press, 1989.

Waterman, Richard W. "The Administrative Presidency, Unilateral Power, and the Unitary Executive Theory." *Presidential Studies Quarterly*, Vol. 39, No. 1 (2009), pp. 5–9.

Whittington, Keith. "Departmentalism, Judicial Supremacy and DACA." *Lawfare*. February 26, 2018.

Will, George F. "The 'Unitary Executive.'" *The Orange County Register*. May 4, 2008.

Wittes, Benjamin and Susan Hennessey. "Is Trump Changing the Executive Branch Forever?" *Foreign Policy*. August 29, 2017.

Wolf, Michael. *Fire and Fury: Inside the Trump White House*. New York: Holt, 2018.

Wurman, Ilan. "Constitutional Administration." *Stanford Law Review*, Vol. 69, No. 359 (2017), pp. 1–61.

Wurman, Ilan. "So, Can the President Obstruct Justice – or Can't He?" *The Hill.* August 7, 2017.

Yoo, Christopher S. "Presidential Power in Historical Perspective." *Journal of Constitutional Law* (2010), pp. 241–150.

Yoo, John C. "An Executive without Much Privilege." *New York Times.* May 25, 2010.

Yoo, John C. "Executive Power Run Amok." *New York Times.* February 6, 2017.

Yoo, John C. "George Washington and the Executive Power." *University of St. Thomas Journal of Law & Public Policy,* Vol. 5, No. 1 (2010), pp. 1–35.

Yoo, John C. "Jefferson and Executive Power." *Boston University Law Review,* Vol. 88 (2008), pp. 421–457.

Yoo, John C. "The Attorneys Hubbub." *Wall Street Journal.* March 22, 2007.

Yoo, John C. "The President's Constitutional Authority to Conduct Military Operations against Terrorists and Nations Supporting Them." (Memorandum to the Deputy Counsel to the President.) September 25, 2001.

Yoo, John C. "Unitary, Executive, or Both?" 76 *University of Chicago Law Review,* Vol. 76, No. 4 (2009), pp. 1935–2018.

Videos (Online)

"The Imperial Presidency and the Founding." Panel at the University of California, Berkeley. (Panelists: Louis Fisher, Jack Rakove, John Yoo, Gordon Silverstein.) September 19, 2008. https://www.youtube.com/watch?v=w1qGDeAZ9-w

"The Unitary Executive through Presidents Bush, Obama, and Trump." Panel at the Federalist Society. (Moderator: Benjamin Wittes; Panelists: Neil Eggleston, Michael Mukasey, Mike Rogers.) May 17, 2017. http://www.fed-soc.org/blog/detail/the-unitary-executive-through-presidents-bush-obama-and-trump